**Personality measures
in admissions**

*Antecedent and personality factors
as predictors of college success*

by Morris I. Stein
New York University

College Entrance Examination Board, New York, 1963

Contents

Foreword iv

Introduction v

The pilot experience 1

The social and demographic approach 7

The psychological approach 16

Current psychological status 22

The transactional approach 50

Summary 55

Conclusion 59

Bibliography 64

Foreword

I want to express my appreciation to Paul F. Lazarsfeld, Quetelet professor of social science, Columbia University, for several invaluable discussions during the period that this monograph was planned and written. To Joshua A. Fishman, dean of the graduate school of education, Yeshiva University; Mrs. Ann K. Pasanella, assistant director of research, College Entrance Examination Board; Isidor Chein, professor of psychology, New York University; Paul S. Burnham, director, office of educational research, Yale University; and Harold Webster, associate research psychologist, Center for the Study of Higher Education, University of California, I am grateful for various comments and suggestions. I am also indebted to Agnes M. Niyekawa, post-doctoral fellow, New York Psychiatric Institute, for her assistance in surveying the literature. And to my secretary, Mrs. Eleanor Cunningham, I want to express my gratitude for her attention to the numerous details involved in preparing the manuscript for publication.

In addition, I would like to express my appreciation to the College Entrance Examination Board for the generous grant which made the preparation of this monograph possible.

Morris I. Stein, director
Research Center for Human Relations
New York University

Introduction

For most colleges the probabilities are 50-50 or less that an entering student will graduate (Iffert, 1956). Consequently, if it were possible to predict early "what kind of person is likely to have what kind of success in what kind of college" (Lazarsfeld, in Barton, 1961), much saving would result in time, money, energy, emotional wear and tear on the student, his family, the faculty, and society at large.*

The need is obvious. Efforts to cope with it, however, have, with few exceptions, met with little success. For the past 40 or 50 years correlations between intellectual predictors and college success have hovered around .50. When antecedent and personality factors are used as sole predictors the situation is hardly better. And, when the latter are combined with intellective predictors, the gain in the multiple correlation is minimal (Fishman, 1961).

In the hope of developing more effective means of coping with the prediction problem a review of a sample of the literature published during the decade, 1950-1960, was undertaken. This sample was limited to studies of the relationships between antecedent and personality factors and some criterion of college success.

A cursory examination of this literature indicated that it was characterized by much diversity. Studies differed from each other in criteria, procedures, characteristics of students studied, the extent to which basic data were reported, and so forth. In view of this diversity and in view of the shortcomings in reporting that make comparisons between studies impossible, it was decided that this monograph might have greater heuristic value if it were organized around the major research approaches or strategies that have been employed rather than if it attempted to organize the literature in terms of content, technique, and so forth.

With this in mind, four different approaches were gleaned from the literature: *the pilot experience, the social or demographic approach, the psychological approach*, and *the transactional approach*.

In the pilot experience approach the investigator selects an experience in the life history of the student that in microcosm possesses characteristics that are most similar to the college experience. This is the student's experience in high school and predictions of college success are based on achievements in high school. The second approach, the social or demographic approach, concentrates on the student's past life history or most specifically on his antecedent characteristics as defined by the characteristics of his

---

*"One-half of the students who graduate in the upper half of the high school classes do not go on to college on a full-time basis and one-third from the upper half do not go to college at all. . . . In terms of national manpower deprivation this means that during the past ten years approximately 1,500,000 students who graduated in the upper half of their high school classes never registered as full-time college students. About 116,000 students who graduated in the top fifth of high school classes in the decade never attended college. This number represents 55 per cent of the full-time faculty of all higher educational institutions in the United States" (Iffert, 1956).

parents or of those situations over which he has had no control. The third approach, the psychological approach, concentrates on the psychological characteristics of the students as manifest in psychological tests administered prior to or early in the college experience. The last of the four approaches is the transactional approach, which is based on the assumption that prediction is a function of the relationships between the students and the college environment. Unlike the other approaches this one emphasizes the importance of understanding the factors that make up the criterion from which one may then derive the characteristics that students need to possess if they are to attain it. The transactional approach also differentiates between a criterion and a standard of performance. The latter is the standard designated by significant persons as representing college success—what is usually called a criterion—whereas the criteria are the students' psychological characteristics.*

In what follows, the assumptions underlying each of the four approaches will be discussed. The approaches will also be illustrated with examples culled from the literature and in this manner some of the substantive data in this area will be presented. But more importantly, as each approach is discussed our attention will be directed to the extent to which it

———
*These approaches, especially the first three, should not be confused with the assessment methods described in *Methods in Personality Assessment* (Stern, Stein, and Bloom, 1956). Those described here are best limited to the area of antecedent and personality characteristics while those described in *Methods* are applicable to the whole assessment area.

fosters the attainment of two goals of all research—understanding and prediction.

Most often, research in this area is evaluated in terms of its contribution to prediction. But prediction that is based on, or results in, relatively little understanding is rather limited. Prediction with understanding contributes to a variety of areas. It tells us more about the characteristics of students who achieve a criterion of academic success and, for those who do not achieve the criterion, it provides data that may be useful in future planning. It helps resolve some of the problems in selecting students for college and furthers the development of firm bases for predictive outcomes. It provides feedback for faculty and college administrators on those factors that make up the criterion and it also provides them with data for counseling students. Finally, it provides an effective basis for developing teaching techniques that are congruent with the students' needs and characteristics.

Thus, there are three major themes in this monograph. The first consists of the four major approaches to prediction, the second is the substantive characteristics that have been studied, and the third is the extent to which they contribute to understanding and prediction.

There are two other points that need to be made explicit at the outset.

Although this monograph concerns itself with approaches to the prediction problem and in that sense is methodological in character, it also deals with substantive material relative to the significance of antecedent and personality factors in academic success. When such substantive material is dealt with, it should not be assumed that intellectual factors have been omitted because they are assumed to be of little or even of secondary importance. Such assumptions would only perpetuate old intraprofessional rivalries. These internecine conflicts are more likely to satisfy personal predilections rather than further our understanding of the basic issues or facilitate our efforts at prediction. Obviously, intellectual, antecedent, and personality factors are all important in understanding individuals. Additional knowledge in all three areas is necessary for predictive purposes.

The second point is that intellectual, antecedent, and personality factors tell us only about the individual. Behavior, however, is a function of the transactional relationships between the individual and his environment. The prediction of college success, therefore, depends on our knowledge of the students, the characteristics of the colleges they attend, and the transactional relationships between the two. In three of the approaches discussed, college characteristics are not considered explicitly but at times they may be inferred from psychological data collected from students. It is only in the transactional approach that a college's characteristics are explicitly considered. Therefore, the reader should be forewarned that to the extent that I have accepted the transactional point of view (Stern, Stein, and Bloom, 1956) I may have done some injustice to the three other approaches—the pilot experience, the social and demographic approach, and the psychological approach—each of which I regard as partial solutions to the prediction problem.

The pilot experience

One approach to the prediction of college success—that which I shall call the pilot experience—is to select an experience in the life history of the student that is most similar to the one he is to have in college and to predict his success in college on the basis of his achievement in the prior experience. The high school experience satisfies this condition best. Both high school and college extend over a period of four years, teachers in both situations are assumed to look for the same kinds of behaviors, and functions involved in learning high school material are regarded as not too dissimilar from those involved in learning college material.

In this strategy high school grades or ranks are utilized as predictors of college success. Although one might think that a student's grades are based on his teacher's subjective judgments, and therefore are likely to be unreliable, this does not turn out to be the case. It has been pointed out "that grade averages may have a reliability as high as +.85, which is not very different from the reliability figures for some of the best aptitude and achievement tests." Although students may differ in achievement and motivation "high school teachers do make relatively precise judgments of students and . . . these judgments are highly related to judgments made by college teachers and to the results of achievement measures" (Bloom and Peters, 1961).

Compared to other types of predictors, the evidence is quite clear that achievement in high school is the best single predictor of college sucess. This conclusion is based not only on recent research but also on a review of much of the past literature. In 1949 Travers reviewed over 200 prediction studies and concluded that average high school grades surpass either subject-matter or psychological tests as predictors of college grades. Their value has also been supported in the recent literature by Altman (1959), Bendig and Klugh (1956), Boyd (1955), Gerritz (1956), Hood (1957), Knaak (1957), and Sie (1955). Not only do high school grades predict grades during the first year of college rather well but they also rank among the best predictors of future college success (Fishman, 1957). However, they may not do so well in predicting the quality of major field of work (French, 1958) undertaken by the student in his college years.

In addition to grades, rank in high school graduating class has also been found to be related to college success. "In general, it can be said that students from the top fifth of a high school class will survive twice as long as students from the bottom fifth. The students graduating from the second fifth in the high school class have 22 per cent better survival prospects than those graduating from the fourth fifth" (Iffert, 1956).

One of the factors that has limited the predictive value of grades is the variability in grading standards used in different high schools. A recent contribution by Bloom and Peters (1961) deals with this problem and yields remarkable results. Using two methods, an internal method and an aptitude method to adjust for differences between high schools, they present correlations between high school and college grades that reach the +.70 level and the +.80 level. In some colleges correlations as high as +.85 have been obtained. These correlations exceed the usual predictive level of +.50 achieved by intellective factors alone. Bloom and Peters are so optimistic about their results that they expect no improvement in the reported correlations unless grading procedures are improved. Furthermore, they also anticipate that "the variance to be accounted for by new aptitude tests, personality indicators of academic achievement, and other instruments is greatly reduced."

The pilot experience approach, therefore, has yielded very good predictors of college success. But grades, considered in and of themselves, provide little understanding either of what it takes to achieve in high school or in college. Consequently, they are of limited value in coping with certain problems and they fall short of providing college administrators and educators with information that may enhance the value of the college experience for the student.

If high school grades are used for selection purposes with relatively little understanding of the characteristics of the students, an adaptation phenomenon may soon develop. College classes selected solely in terms of students who have achieved well in high school may become quite homogeneous in this characteristic and with this increased homogeneity and with differential grading systems one would expect the predictive correlations to fall, and the problem would be reopened for further investigation.

The second shortcoming of the pilot experience approach is the "lag phenomenon." Predictions based on grades are dependent on experiences with specific high schools. The pilot experience strategy is very empirical and no guide lines are presented for dealing with new schools and new situations. Consequently, with the increase in size of population attending high school and thus the increase in new high schools, the pilot experience can become effective only some time after students from specific high schools have been accepted at specific colleges.

The third major problem with the pilot experience approach is that it does not allow for change in the individual. For example, it cannot cope with the problem of the "late bloomers," those students who manifest a rather rapid growth in maturation only during the late years of high school or individuals who might profit later from college stimulation. Change in the individual may occur as a result of chance factors, maturational processes in the individual, and as a result of exposure to new stimuli and new situations.

Some of the shortcomings in the pilot experience approach might be overcome if studies of the personality characteristics of high grade achievers were undertaken. One of the best efforts in this direction is the work of Holland and his study of a rather select segment of the student population.

What are the characteristics of the student who achieves high high school rank? To answer this question Holland (1960) studied 148 boys and 140 girls who constituted a representative sample of a larger population of finalists in the National Merit Scholarship program.

For this sample he correlated 40 predictors with high school rank. The predictors included the Scholastic Aptitude Test of the College Entrance Examination Board (SAT), the Cattell 16 Personality Factors (PF), the NMSS (an experimental personality inventory), the VPI (an experimental personality inventory composed of occupational titles), and a teacher rating of "maturity."

Analysis of the data "imply that the boy with high HSR (high school rank) is characterized by a number of personal traits in addition to his drive to achieve academically. For instance, he is often rated high by his teachers. . . . He appears to be somewhat feminine (dislikes physical activity), serious (as opposed to playful), conservative, aspiring, responsible, persistent, and intelligent. The correlates for girls suggest that high HSR is associated with submissiveness (also unsociability), self-control, intelligence, self-deprecation, passivity, intellectuality, and self-sufficiency." Briefly, "These correlates indicate then that HSR is a function of high academic aptitude, an academic personality syndrome, and positive relationships with teachers."

If these are the personality correlates of HSR what are the personality correlates of college achievement? Using a sample of 641 boys and 311 girls drawn from 7,500 finalists in the National Merit Scholarship program, Holland correlated their freshman grades in college, or honor point ratio, against all the variables used in the previous study with the exception of teachers' ratings on maturity and found "that the college achiever has done well in high school (HSR) and has high scholastic aptitude. The non-intellectual predictors . . . characterize the male achiever as dependent, serious (not playful), persistent, responsible, submissive, quiet . . . feminine, naïve, self-sufficient, and self-controlled. The female achiever is characterized as persistent, responsible, submissive . . . and conservative."

Combining the data of these two studies, it is apparent that those characteristics that are correlated with high school rank "are generally the best predictors of college grades." Furthermore, these factors are very similar to those found by Holland (1959a) in a previous study when he used a different test of personality (the California Psychological Inventory) and found that on this test those scales that were the best predictors of college success were: Socialization, Social Presence, and Self-Control.

In other words, Holland's studies indicate that the student who achieves high high school rank or who achieves high grades at least during the first year in college is very much the socialized individual who is unlikely to express very much of his own individuality. Now this is the kind of student that educators and administrators may wish to accept and produce but, if so, it is at variance with educational principles that purportedly emphasize the importance of autonomy, freeing the potentiality of the individual, and encouraging his creativity.

The extent to which the personality picture of the

student, who achieves high high school rank and high grades at least during the first year of college, deviates from the personality picture of the creative adult is also a topic to which Holland addresses himself. It will be recalled that in one of Holland's (1960) studies the Cattell 16 PF test had been used. Cattell and his co-workers (Cattell and Drevdahl, 1955; Drevdahl, 1956; Drevdahl and Cattell, 1958) had previously used this test in studies of creativity among adults. These studies, as summarized by Holland (1960), describe "the 'creative' person as intelligent, emotionally mature, dominant, adventurous, emotionally sensitive (feminine), introverted, radical, self-sufficient, tense, unsociable, depressive, less subject to group standards, and impulsive . . ." Although Cattell's subjects are not comparable to Holland's students in terms of age and other factors it is nevertheless tenable, at least as an initial hypothesis, that if high schools were rewarding creativity that the personality characteristics associated with high grades in high school or the first year of college might be similar to or the same as those obtained by Cattell and his co-workers. A comparison of the personality characteristics found by Holland and those found by Cattell indicates that this is not so. Holland (1960) makes this point stand out in bold relief when he says, "Only two of the 16 PF scales indicative of creative potential are correlated with grades in the expected direction—emotionally sensitive, feminine, and surgent—while five scales are significantly correlated with grades in directions which suggest a lack of creative potential and the remaining five scales

characteristic of 'more creative' people are not significantly related to grades. The implication that the college achiever has less potential for creative activity is supported by our findings about the correlates of HSR." This finding is further supported by another study of Holland's (1959b) in which he investigated the personality correlates of teachers' ratings of maturity with the 16 PF scales and also found that students with high HSR "may have less creative potential than students with low HSR, assuming that the latter also have other attributes associated with creative behavior." And then there is MacKinnon's (1959c) study in which he reports that creative research scientists and architects had undistinguished college grades.

Finally, and the point cannot be made better than Holland (1960) himself does, "The implications of the present investigation, which are consistent with our growing knowledge of creativity, argue against the uncritical use of high school and college grades as predictors of post-college achievement and as unqualified criteria for selecting persons for admissions, scholarships, fellowships, or jobs. Similarly the prediction of college grades appears to be an increasingly dubious research enterprise. It seems preferable to develop more valid criteria of independent achievement and creativity, even though colleges may not recognize and reward these tendencies. To continue the prediction of college grades only reinforces their somewhat specious validity and delays the development of more adequate criteria and the subsequent re-examination of educational goals and practices."

Using Holland's results, our knowledge of what it takes to achieve well in both high school and college is increased over that which would have been available to us had we been limited solely to predicting from high school grades. This added information is important in two respects. It has methodological significance and it provides significant feedback for college administrators and educators. Methodologically, it alerts investigators attempting to predict college success to the fact that they should not succumb to various clichés about college education—that it frees the individual for independent pursuits and brings to the fore his individuality and uniqueness—(unless they find this to be true in specific colleges studied). Rather, the investigator needs to be aware of the possibility that in our present society, a college education may be a continuation of the socialization (rather than the individuation) process. If one is to be successful in college, by certain criteria, it helps if one is willing to submerge one's own individuality to the pressures of conformity, at least for the early college years, if not for the duration of the college experience. In this context high school grades may well be regarded as being in part measures of how well socialized or compliant the individual has been up to a certain point in his life, and they may be predictive of how well he will continue to be socialized.

There is another interesting aspect in Holland's data. They highlight for us an important dynamic relationship between personality and learning. Learning may be an end in itself where the individual enjoys the learning experience in and of itself or he enjoys the experience of successfully solving problems for their own ends. Learning, however, may also be a *means* to an end. It may subserve other needs. Holland's data suggest that if conformity makes for college success then the college experience may be regarded not as an end itself (on which other growth-oriented goals might be built) but rather as a means to an end. The end may be "to get the degree," "to get college over with," so that one might engage in other pursuits. College may be regarded by successful students as a staying action, or to be put up with as any other initiation rite until one can strike out on his own. These extreme, or possibly not so extreme, cases are cited to suggest the meaning of college for some students. In so doing, one should not overlook the possibility that there are other students who no doubt profit more from the college experience in the direction of self-growth. One of the problems of future research is to distinguish between the two groups.

The statements made above are obviously contingent on the criterion of college success—grades. The relationship between conformity and college success might also be derived from an analysis of grades as a criterion.

The criterion used in Holland's study was honor point ratio. To obtain it, "All grades were converted by an honor point ratio formula where A = 4, B = 3, C = 2, D = 1, F = 0 grades were multiplied by credits per course and divided by total credits carried." Unfortunately, Holland does not present data on the different number of courses that make up the criterion of college success. However, Burnham (1962) presents interesting information in this regard. He says, "thirty years ago the members of the freshman class (at Yale) might be enrolled in something like 20 courses, in a total of 12 to 15 departments. The present freshman class is represented in some 148 different courses in some 39 different departments." Whether this is typical of other college students is not known but from it one might well assume that honor point ratios are currently based on a rather wide sampling of courses. To be able to achieve high honor point ratios might therefore indicate that the student is a "Renaissance man"—he is a well-rounded, cultured, and possibly creative individual, a genius. Or at the other extreme it might mean that he has the capacity to pass courses without regard to their significance to him as an individual with specific interests.

The personality data associated with high college grades are also of potential feedback value to college administrators. Using these data as a base one might ask them, "Do you want to continue to risk producing conforming individuals by rewarding behavior associated with high grades? In view of the predictive efficiency of high school grades, are you willing to view college as a duplication of, or as a possibly minor extension of, the high school experience? Are the values presently extant in most colleges congruent with producing adults who might make significant contributions to society in the future?" The research presented cannot provide answers to these questions but they can restimulate the need for further questioning about educational goals. And, if and when changes are instituted, psychological tests can be of further help as indicators of how well educators have come to achieving their goals.

The social and demographic approach

The social and demographic approach is manifest in those investigations in which the relationship of characteristics of others with whom the student has been associated or reared (parents' socioeconomic status, professional status, or education) or factors over which he has had no control (urban-rural residence, birth order) are related to college success. The variables selected for study are taken over from other studies in social research where they have proven valuable. In so doing it is assumed that these variables are related to the student's predispositions, attitudes, values, and expectancies as they have been found to be so related in other social research. Whether the student actually possesses these characteristics is seldom tested directly. Nevertheless, when differentiating results are found they are usually interpreted in a *post hoc* fashion using the findings of other studies for interpretation.

This approach as it is currently used is largely empirical. Hypotheses are rarely tested and the suggested relationships based on the empirical findings are rarely cross-validated.

Age, sex, birth order, religious and ethnic affiliation, parents' educational and professional status, rural and urban residence are some of the variables investigated in the studies that make up this approach. The types of results obtained follow.

Age. Age does not bear a linear relationship to college success. It is dependent on the continuity of the educational experience. Where students have had a continuous educational record, that is, where they continued on to college directly from high school, the younger the student the more likely is he to be successful in college (Hood, 1957; MacLachlan and Burnett, 1954; Mukherjee, 1958; and Patton, 1958). This, however, is not always the case (Bergeron, 1953). By contrast, where students delayed their college education, older students are more likely to be more successful than younger students (Bledsoe, 1953).

It is possible that the greater success of the younger student may be ascribed to the fact that he has greater intellectual capacity and has demonstrated his intellectual precocity previously in elementary and high school. It might also be that when he enters college he is too young to participate in and be distracted by extracurricular activities and thus concentrates more on his studies. The discontinuous older student returning to complete his education after he has been in the outside world may see greater significance in the value of education possibly for vocational or professional achievement and may therefore have a more structured definition of the college experience and a greater commitment to it.

Sex. Gerritz (1956) found female students to be more successful at the University of Minnesota than males. They had higher honor point ratios. Using seven college samples including 3,546 students, Abelson (1951) found that college grades for females are more predictable from high school grades or from high school grades used in combination with aptitude test scores, not because of "the higher validity of (the) predictors for girls than for boys . . . (but because of) the greater homogeneity of girls' college grades; that is, the standard deviation of college grades was smaller for the girls than it was for the boys."

Some understanding of how sex difference may contribute to the prediction problem is offered by the work of Weitz and his colleagues. In one study (Weitz and Wilkinson, 1957) they found that male students who express a preference for a major field achieve a higher quality point average than those who do not. For female students the trend is in the same direction but the result is not statistically significant. In a later study, Weitz and Colver (1959) concentrated on female students and examined in further detail the differences between girls who did and those who did not have educational goals. They concluded that girls perform equally well in the academic environment whether or not they had clearly defined educational goals. Female students, they suggest, come to college to secure an education and the content of the education seems to have little bearing on their performance.

Hood (1957) studied entering freshmen at Cornell University with an extensive questionnaire that included questions on personal and family history, educational background, personal philosophies, college expectancies, and relationships with others. Several years later he compared the responses of those who did not complete two consecutive years of college with those who did and found that different fac-

tors were related to attrition for boys and for girls.

For female students, those "who were 'engaged or going steady' or who came from small home towns, had significantly higher attrition rates. Those who expected to be popular with many acquaintances in college as opposed to having just a few close friends and those who reported a higher frequency of leadership in the past, tended to have a lower attrition rate."

For male students Hood found that "age, occupational level of father, educational level of father, and rank in secondary school varsity athletics were found to be significantly related to dropping out in a manner consistent with the findings of other studies. Those who reportedly spent longer than average amounts of time on their secondary school homework dropped out in significantly larger numbers." In males who had higher attrition rates it was also found that they expected greater satisfaction in their future careers as against family relationships and they "felt that the most important requirement of their profession would be to earn a good deal of money or to provide security as opposed to providing an opportunity to work with people or to be helpful to them." Finally, males who sought friendships with upperclassmen (as opposed to fellow freshmen), males who hoped to develop their own personalities (as opposed to those who hoped to improve their ability to deal with people), and males who did not know whether it was healthy to disagree with their parents and who said "don't know" to questions about parental attitudes and opinions also had higher attrition rates.

From the above it is apparent that sex is a contingency variable and that different variables and different formulas are necessary to predict the academic achievements of males and females.

Birth order. Only-children were found to have a significantly higher grade-point average during their first semester at college than did a control group (Weitz and Wilkinson, 1957). Unfortunately, there is no direct test as to why this should be so. If one assumes that conformity behavior may be involved in obtaining higher grades, then Schachter's work (1959) may help explain some of the results. Schachter says that, "Independent measures of dependence prove to be systematically related to ordinal position, with first-born individuals consistently more dependent than later-born individuals. Influencibility, which is assumed to be in part a function of dependence, is demonstrated to be related to ordinal position. It is anticipated that other dependency-linked behaviors will eventually prove to be related to ordinal position."

There may be a relationship between birth order and family size but the data are thus far contradictory. Peterson (1958) reports that oldest children in a family of four or more children dropped out of college more frequently than other children. But Carter and McGinnis (1952) report that number of children in the family did not differentiate between students with highest and lowest honor point ratio. Among other factors, we do not know from these studies the relationship between number of children in the family and the family's financial means to support the student in college.

Religious and ethnic status. Gerritz (1956) found a larger proportion of Jewish students in the upper 27 per cent of the distribution of honor point ratios than of students of other religious affiliations. And Hood (1957) found tentative evidence to suggest that students who did not complete two consecutive years of college, in contrast to those who did, either had very strong and rigid religious values or a complete absence of religious faith. Thus, possibly it is not the student's specific religious affiliation but rather the intensity of his value or belief system which may be the significant variable.

Parents' characteristics. A series of studies have gathered information on parents and related these to students' achievement.

Academically successful students, it has been found, come from families where fathers hold upper-level occupations—generally professional or managerial (Gerritz, 1956; Hood, 1957; MacLachlan and Burnett, 1954; Mukherjee, 1958; Patton, 1958).

Parents' birthplace has also been investigated and in one study (Myers, 1950) in an eastern women's liberal arts college it was found that having parents of whom one or both were foreign born was related to achievement. And in another study (Gerritz, 1956), it was found that fathers being foreign born was associated with success. Both these studies were conducted at state universities.

Hood (1957) found father's educational level to be inversely related to attrition among his male students but not among his female students. Educational level of the mother has also figured in research. Thus Mukherjee (1958) compared honor students with a random sample of students from the same class and found that while two-thirds of the fathers of honor students had received a high school education this percentage was larger when the mother's educational status was considered. Carter and McGinnis (1952) comparing 100 students with highest point hour ratio with 100 students who had lowest point hour ratio found that the fact that the mother did not graduate from high school is far more significant in predicting college failure than the fact that the father did or did not graduate from high school or that either parent did or did not attend or graduate from college.

With regard to family income, Iffert (1956), in his study of drop-outs, reports that financial limitations are not the only considerations in affecting the length of time a student will stay in school. "It is true," he says, "that nearly half (48.9 per cent) of the students who drop out during or at the end of the first registration period came from homes in which the family income was under $5,000." However, "About one-sixth (16.5 per cent) of the first-registration drop-outs come from the $10,000 and higher income group." Considering the reasons students give for dropping out of school, Iffert finds that academic difficulties are more serious than financial ones during the first year but the reverse is true for those who drop out after the first year. On the basis of these findings Iffert recommends re-examination of scholarship policies by suggesting, "I hope it is not too harsh to say that the indiscriminate use of scholar-

ships to lure freshmen to the campus depletes funds that could be better used to hold students of demonstrated ability."

Urban-rural factors. Although urban and "mixed" groups were found to be superior to rural groups on standardized measures of aptitude and achievement, the three groups do not differ significantly among themselves on measures of scholastic attainment based on college grades (Sanders, *et al.*, 1955). Nor are urban-rural factors as useful prognostically as high school rank or test scores (Boyd, 1955).

Urban-rural factors may operate in a contingency fashion when combined with sex. Thus, Hood (1957), as reported previously, found that among female students those coming from smaller towns had higher attrition rates.

Private versus public school attendance. One of the differentiating characteristics of high schools is whether they are publicly or privately supported. Presumably, privately supported schools, on the assumption that they are financially capable, are in a better position to provide their students with more individual attention in smaller classes. The curriculum is also likely to be enriched and the students might be more likely to be more successful in their college experiences than students who come from public schools where presumably students have not experienced the advantages of such attention and enrichment. Obviously all these assumptions are based on stereotypes, and the critical factors are whether or not these characteristics do obtain, rather than whether the school is privately or publicly supported.

Indeed, as we shall see, the evidence indicates that public school students are frequently more successful in college than are private school students. But from an educational point of view even this datum is not as critical as the fact that the students going to these two types of schools are likely to differ sufficiently in types of personal backgrounds and are rather different from each other in psychological makeup. Therefore, predictions have to be made on different factors for each of the groups.

Mohandessi and Runkel (1958) found that private high schools had a higher mean academic aptitude than public schools as measured by differential aptitude tests in a statewide testing program in Illinois. At Princeton University, Davis and Frederiksen (1955) found that public school graduates made higher academic averages during their freshman year in relation to their academic ability than did private school graduates. The same was found to be true during their sophomore years. At Vassar College, private and public school attendance did not differentiate between "potentially superior" and "potentially not superior" students (Brown, 1960) according to judgments of faculty.

Audrey Shuey (1956, 1958) reports two studies from Randolph-Macon Woman's College in which she sought to determine whether the differences between private and public school students would obtain over the first two years of college life. Her first study was conducted with students when they were freshmen and on the basis of this research she says, "it would appear that public school students earned higher grades, on the average, than the students from private schools who were of the same age, intelligence, with similar academic programs, from the same section of the country, and from communities of similar size" (Shuey, 1958). Furthermore, the two groups did not differ significantly from each other in religious preference, number of children in the family, parents' education, percentages of broken homes, or participation in extracurricular activities.

Shuey then concluded that the higher public school means might be attributed to the following factors: students from public schools have a greater need to prove themselves during their first year away from home, they accept the belief that private school students are better prepared for college, or they were less dependent on strict parental supervision in precollege years. These factors, Shuey felt, might be much more potent in the freshman year than in subsequent years. Therefore, a second study was undertaken in which the achievements of 245 pairs of private and public school students were studied during their sophomore year. This population was selected from the total sophomore groups that had been in attendance at Randolph-Macon during a nine-year period. It also included all those who had been part of the freshman-year study and who had gone on to their sophomore year. Additional pairs of students were added to substitute for those in the freshman year study who had dropped out.

The sophomore students were matched on: American Council on Education Psychological Examination (ACE) scores ±5 points, section of the country, and size of the community or city from which they came. The groups were also approximately equal in age, had taken courses of similar levels of difficulty, were equal in intelligence test scores, academic load, and equal in the number contributing to self-support.

Since many of the students included in the freshman-year study were also part of the sophomore study, certain comparisons could be made. The two groups of sophomores had lost about the same number of students at the end of the freshman year. Qualitatively, however, the public school group suffered the greater loss, for the quality point ratios of the public school drop-outs were higher than the mean of the freshmen as a group, whereas the reverse was true for the private school students who dropped out. Therefore, Shuey says, the public school group could not be regarded as a more highly selected group during their sophomore year.

Nevertheless, the results of this second study confirmed those of the first. Again, public school students earned significantly higher grades than did private school students. In view of this confirmation, Shuey suggests that the continued superiority of the public school students during the freshman year could not be attributed to their being accustomed to less supervision in studying or to their being more highly motivated in their first year away from home. Rather, Shuey concludes that public school students are either better prepared for college or that college admissions officers give more weight to the grades and class standing of public school applicants than they do to those of private school students.

Weitz and Wilkinson (1957) did not find that private and public school students earned significantly different grade-point averages during their first semester. However, military school graduates did receive significantly higher grades than non-military school graduates. They therefore suggest that in studies where differences between private and public schools were not found it may have been because military and non-military private preparatory schools were combined.

Probably the best summary of the differences between private and public school students has been presented by McArthur (1960). He does not postulate that the schools "cause" the personalities of their students, but rather that self and social selection factors are likely to be involved.

McArthur points to the fact that it has been demonstrated that public school students outperform private school students even when IQ is held constant. Furthermore, these relationships hold in the face of the upward shift in all grades brought about by the depression, and they hold up even when the measure predicting scholastic aptitude includes previous grades. McArthur suggests that there may be differences between the groups in levels of aspiration. He bases this on the fact that even when previous under and over-achieving status have been allowed for, the public school boys continue to overachieve in college while the private school boys continue to underachieve. Thus, the two groups "find the same relative levels even when the absolute level of the task changes greatly."

The meaning of the IQ is also different for the two groups of students. With the same IQ, private school boys will have more intellectual range and power for their speed, while public school boys will have more speed for their range and power.

When IQ is held constant, public school and private school boys also differ in cognitive style. For example, on the Rorschach Test, public school boys are long on quantity and accuracy while private school boys are long on quality. The latter, McArthur points out, "don't give many responses, often as few as one to a blot. What they do is to elaborate and embroider that one response, working in all facets of the problem presented by the blot before they are willing to let the response stand."

Need achievement scores (measured by McClelland's pictures or by Murray's Thematic Apperception Test) predict the public school graduates' college grades but not the grades of private school students.

An 18-year follow-up study with the Strong Vocational Interest Blank (VIB) indicated that it predicted well the public school students' careers but predicted very little about the future of the private school students. For the latter, the best predictor was simply to ask them, while in college, what they were going to be doing 20 years later. An item analysis of the Strong VIB indicated, "that public school boys choose items that have to do with success and science, while private school students choose clusters of social, aesthetic, statusful, and romantic outdoor activity items." McArthur suggests that, "It was as though these young men had read Parsons on ascribed *vs.* achieved status and then filled out their Strongs accordingly."

On a test of authoritarianism of the 15 lowest scores, all were obtained from public school students, while of the 15 highest scores 12 were obtained from private school students.

Differences in personality were also found between public and private school groups on the Bernreuter and Rorschach Tests. In addition to differences in cognitive style there was evidence for emotional constriction in private school groups. Furthermore, on the Thematic Apperception Test, totally different motives were mediated by totally different childhood experiences.

Finally, McArthur cites the research of Caron and Wallach (1957) on memory, in which it was found that public school students recalled best the tasks they failed to complete, while private school students repressed or suppressed their failures and recalled best their successes.

In summary, then, it may be said that public school students and private school students come from different subcultures. "Not only do members of American subcultures have different traits," McArthur says, "but different dynamics underlie these traits. Not only do they have different memories but they obey different laws of memory. Not only do they have different learnings but these may have been acquired by means of different laws of learning. All of these subcultural effects on personality show up within and between college student populations." Colleges do not cause these differences, but as in any other situation the institutional culture may well reinforce and encourage existing behavior patterns and attitudes.

These, then, are samples of the types of variables investigated and the types of results obtained with the social or demographic approach.

As this approach is currently employed, it has one major advantage. It is relatively simple to gather the data needed for the study. The investigator need only go to the students' records or administer a simple questionnaire inquiring into the social variables that interest him.

The ease of gathering data, however, is overshadowed by certain disadvantages. The approach provides very little direct understanding of the psychological characteristics of the students. As it now stands, it consists of only "one cut" through the data and at that, in terms of the development of the behavioral sciences today, a superficial one. What understanding is developed is generally of a *post hoc* variety. Inferences are drawn not from the data but from accumulated knowledge in other areas in which the same variables have been used. For example, if it is found that students coming from upper-class backgrounds do better in college than those from lower-class backgrounds, it might be suggested that the former had more advantages than the latter or came from a home where the value system of the family might be more congruent with those of the college environment. When lower-class students are found to be more successful, then "upward mobility"

may be invoked as a critical factor. These factors— that is, the advantages and value system of the upper-class group, or the upward mobility of the lower-class group—could have been suggested on the basis of available sociological literature and could have been investigated directly to determine whether the psychological derivatives or concomitants of social factors are indeed relevant to college success, and, if so, under what circumstances. The direct study of values, mobility patterns, and so forth, is also a more relevant approach because these factors do cut across class lines, although, in the generality, they may be more characteristic of one social class than another.

As we have seen, it is also typical of the social and demographic approach that relationships are presented between single social and demographic variables and academic success. Studies using this approach may investigate the relationship between college success and the father's profession or between college success and the student's urban or rural origin, and so forth. When differentiating results are obtained, social or psychological factors (mobility, value on education, and so forth) are inferred. What is overlooked, however, is that two different social events may be functionally equivalent psychologically. Thus, while it may be true in the generality, that an upper or a middle-class child may have values that are congruent with college success because of the stimuli and models to which he has been exposed at home, and a lower-class student may not be regarded as possessing these values due to the socioeconomic status of his parents, it is nevertheless possible that the lower-class student may have taken on these values from other experiences. He may have adopted them if he lived in an urban area from visits to museums, libraries, or from associating with people outside his home who possess values different from his own family.

Similarly, two individuals may be reared in the same situation where presumably they were exposed to what appears to be the same external environment but their reactions to these environments may be quite different. Thus, two students may be reared in a lower-class environment and for one it may result in a rather pessimistic attitude regarding the future, while it may stimulate the achievement orientation of the other. Consequently, it is not the external characteristic of the event which may be significant for college success but its functional significance within the individual's psychological make-up. McArthur's research, cited previously on public and private school students, is a step in this direction.

In concluding the discussion of the social and demographic approach it should be pointed out that in pursuing it one runs some risk of encouraging the development or continuation of stereotypes and prejudices. In this area, research data often cannot be considered apart from their potential social utility. Thus, when data are presented indicating class or ethnic differences, the temptation on the part of admissions officers to select their students on these bases is likely to be strong. Such stereotypic behavior may result in an injustice to the student for he is assumed to possess those characteristics that actually represent or reflect characteristics that have been ascribed to others with whom he has been associated, reared, or over which he has had no control. Is it not more important to attend to the student's own individuality including his abilities and potentialities?

The psychological approach

If it may be said that the social or demographic approach assumes that history makes the man, then it may be said that the psychological approach is based on the assumption that man makes history. Consequently, the psychological approach focuses on the individual's personality characteristics and investigates those which it assumes may either hinder or facilitate his progress in college. In common with the pilot experience and the social or demographic approach, the psychological approach as it has been used has not attempted to clarify the criterion of college success, nor has it directly investigated the forces or characteristics of the college environment that may facilitate or inhibit a student's success. The characteristics of the college environment in most of the studies using this approach are, however, implicit in the data. Since most of these studies concentrate on one college, the college's selection criteria, values, and so forth, are certainly operative but these are not made as explicit as one finds in the transactional approach to be considered later.

To gather data on students' characteristics, a variety of procedures have been used—paper and pencil tests, projective tests, questionnaires, and, to a much lesser extent, experimental situations. In the main, the procedures do not focus on a single personality characteristic but on several. It is apparent that investigators using this approach assume that college populations possess the same large array of personality characteristics and that individuals differ only in degree. One might question, however, whether college students' needs manifest their characteristics in the same environment in the same way.

Let this general description of the psychological approach suffice at this point. We shall return to additional assumptions and descriptions later. The presentation of the psychological approach is divided into two major units. The first concerns itself with the individual's early history and concentrates specifically on parent-child relationships. The examples we shall consider have been developed in the area of creativity but they are also of potential value in studying factors related to college success.

The second unit in this section contains studies that concern themselves with the students' current characteristics and consider such variables as over-all adjustment, anxiety, control and compulsiveness, need achievement, masculinity and femininity, and typological characteristics.

Early history. In discussing the social and demographic approach, especially those studies that concentrate on parents' characteristics, it was pointed out that these studies tell us little about the transactions between parents and students, yet much of the psychological literature would suggest that it is the nature of these transactions and the character of parent-child relationships that are likely to be major influences on the individual's later development. In line with this literature, steps have been taken to investigate these relationships in other areas, especially creativity, which are proving to be of some interest and value and might well be mentioned here for what they might contribute to further our understanding of college success.

Roe's research in the area of creativity has led her to the belief that a knowledge of parent-child relationships may provide much data that could be related to future interests (Roe, 1957). She believes that interests are more important than aptitudes in the choice of later occupations and since interests and aptitudes generally correlate only .30, that more effective work would be possible if better information on interests were available.

Interests for Roe "arise out of the child's earliest experiences in the family. They are determined primarily by the areas in which his attention is given free flow in the family structure and the way in which he is handled in particular situations." As a framework for dealing with the various ways in which the child may be handled in the family, Roe presents a series of critical variables that she represents diagrammatically by a series of concentric circles. At the center is the basic attitude of the family toward children which may be classified on a continuum ranging from warm to cold. This basic attitude may be subdivided into three attitudes toward handling children: (1) "Emotional concentration on the child" (that is, where the child is the primary focus of the parents' concern) which may be expressed in a variety of ways ranging from 'overprotection of the child' to being 'overdemanding' of the child. (2) 'Avoidance' which may be subdivided into 'rejection' and 'neglect' and (3) 'Acceptance' which may be subdivid-

ed into 'casual acceptance' and 'loving acceptance.'"

Roe then hypothesizes that, "the first distinction in basic attitudes which later develops into interests is whether or not your basic orientation is toward persons, while the others have a basic orientation 'not toward persons.'"

The major orientation toward persons can be subdivided into an orientation toward the self as a person or toward other persons and it may be defensive or nondefensive. From this group of individuals, Roe suggests, come those individuals who are "suited to occupations in which the most important element is the relationship of one individual to another. For example, at the upper level of occupations will be personal therapists, vocational guidance people, welfare workers—of one sort or another—social workers, and so on. At the lower level of occupations there will be barbers, beauticians, etc., in which there is a direct personal relationship. You will also get what I call the arts and entertainment group of occupations, where I think a major element is a form of narcissism which derives out of this framework. I do not separate music and painting and other arts, because I think the essential element is the same in them, and I would include big league baseball players, for example, in the same group. Here the narcissism refers to a different sort of body structure than it would in terms of the artist.

"In groups with basic orientation *not toward persons*, there can be an orientation toward things or objects in the environment which may be animate or inanimate, or perhaps toward the ideas, although you will get some orientation of a very limited sort toward ideas in the other previous group. Primarily many scientists—except some social scientists—will come out of this latter group. Obviously, I am generalizing very broadly, and there may be some exceptions.

"In the neglected group and in the casual acceptance group, you will get persons whose basic orientation is not toward persons—in a nondefensive way. I do not agree with the analysts that if you are not basically oriented toward persons it is because of defense against them. I know too many scientists who do not show this, but in whom the primary interest—the thing they think about most easily, the thing they attend to most easily—is a thing or object or animal, not persons. These persons will develop into a technological group, *i.e.*, a biological sciences group, a physical sciences group, etc."

In addition to the hypotheses just presented, Roe also hypothesizes as to why aptitudes and interests do not correlate very highly. Aptitudes, she believes, have a genetic basis primarily but they need the opportunity to come to fruition. Interests, on the other hand, have an experiential basis and they may or may not coincide with aptitudes. Using the previously described framework for gathering data, Roe believes that the group of individuals among whom we might find those persons who do have a greater correlation between interests and aptitudes are those who come from the acceptance groups. In the families of these individuals there are no pressures on them either for or against checking out their aptitudes. "They manifest an aptitude and they get a chance to try it out—

either because nobody is paying too close attention to them or because it is part of the philosophy of their parents to give them a chance to develop this aptitude without trying to be too guiding about it."

With regard to creativity, Roe says that among individuals with a major orientation toward persons it is more difficult to get free flowing creativity than from individuals whose major orientation is not toward persons. Among the former, creativity is likely to occur on a defensive basis. "I was rather surprised to find," she says, "in some of my studies of physical scientists particularly, a freedom and ease of working creatively, much more than I found in the social scientists, rather more than I found in the biological scientists, and I think considerably more than I found in the artists I studied. The artists usually got themselves into a terrific stew just before they were about to create something. To some extent this stirred-up condition happens in scientists, but I think it occurs to a lesser extent and has a different quality."

These are examples of some hypotheses suggested by Roe. Indeed, much more research needs to be done in terms of the framework she suggests. Even in its rough outline it appears potentially quite fruitful as a means of increasing our understanding about the development of interests and their relationships with other factors. It is also potentially fruitful as a means of predicting styles of behavior and success in different areas of occupational and professional choice whose requirements may or may not be congruent with interest patterns developed by an individual in the course of his development.

Stein and his co-workers (unpublished) have also been interested in the psychological meaningfulness of parent-child relationships, especially as they may relate to creativity in adult life. To gather their data two questionnaires were developed. One of these is a rather complete autobiographical form and another devotes itself solely to interpersonal relationships in childhood seen retrospectively. Examples of questions asked follow. The results that are presented are based on information obtained from 33 "more" and 34 "less" creative (defined in terms of ratings obtained from their supervisors, colleagues, and subordinates) Ph.D. chemists employed in industrial research organizations.

To gather information on parents' interests in this study, the men were presented with several interest areas and asked to check which of them was of interest to each of their parents. The categories were:

a. Music, painting, literature, and other artistic areas.

b. Science (read about the different sciences, read science fiction, went to museums, had a laboratory, telescope, and so forth).

c. Business (concerned primarily with job, career, or office, making money, investments, and so forth).

d. Family (concerned primarily with the family, how the children were doing in school, how they were getting along with others, spent a good deal of time with spouse and children).

e. Sports and outdoor activity (engaged in sports or was a sports fan).

f. Social (enjoyed being with his friends for conversations, card playing, or just to pass the time of day, belonging to lodges, clubs, and associations).

g. Workshop (enjoyed making things around the house, making toys, fixing up the house, and so forth).

h. Politics (took part in local or national politics; was an avid reader of current political events on the local, national, and international scene).

i. Was not interested in any of the activities listed.

On the average, the fathers of the more creative group were said to have had more interests (5.1) than did those of the less creative group (4.3). The mothers of both groups had the same number of interests (3.5 and 3.0, respectively). Thus the fathers had more interests than the mothers, and the parents of the more creative men tended to have more interests than the parents of the less creative men. The one interest which distinguished the fathers of the more creative men was their interest in science. While 18 per cent of the fathers of the less creative men were said to be interested in science, this was true of 45 per cent of the fathers of the more creative men (and by no means were 45 per cent of the fathers of more creative men scientists). The mothers, on the other hand, were differentiated only by their interest in business. While only 12 per cent of the mothers of the less creative men were said to be interested in business, this was true of 35 per cent of the mothers of the more creative men.

Data were also sought on the types of goals that the parents had for their sons. The men were presented with six types of goals and asked to indicate which of them were held by the father and which were held by the mother. The men were also asked to indicate which of these goals they felt they had achieved.

The six types of goals were:

1. Business—to make money, or become a business man, or both.

2. Scholarship (including science)—to be scholarly and learned, or to become a scientist, or both.

3. Social—to do good for people and to be liked by them.

4. Religious—to be religious, or work for a religious cause, or both.

5. Political—to be well informed in politics, or to become involved in political affairs, or both.

6. Aesthetic—to be interested in the arts, or to become an artist, musician, and so forth, or both.

Some of the results obtained were: In 94 per cent of the cases of the more creative group both parents *did* hold goals for their sons compared to 70 per cent of the less creative men. Both parents had *no* goals in one case of the more creative group and in 21 per cent of the less creative group.

The most frequently mentioned goal for all parents was scholarship and science. It occurred for 65 per cent of the fathers and 68 per cent of the mothers of the more creative group and for 48 per cent of the fathers and 61 per cent of the mothers in the less creative group.

In addition to the value system of the home, Stein and his co-workers also investigated their subjects' recollections of their relationships with their parents during childhood. To gather the necessary data, a questionnaire developed by Shanan and Stein, called the IRC (Interpersonal Relations in Childhood), was used. Among the areas covered by the questionnaire were the subjects' recollections of how they perceived their parents, how they felt in their parents' presence, the extent to which they identified with either of their parents, and the areas in which they wanted to be either similar to or different from their parents. To indicate their responses, subjects were presented with a series of adjective pairs on which they could check the frequency of their reactions or the intensity of their perceptions. The pairs were not presented as the polar extremes of a continuum. Rather, the subject was asked to react to each adjective separately. For example, the subject was asked to indicate how strongly he perceived each parent both as warm and as cold. The scoring system is such that the adjective pairs may also be regarded as if they were the extremes of a continuum.

Here is a sample of the findings. (These are based on the same group of individuals considered previously except that the number of more creative subjects is decreased by one.) A significantly larger proportion of more creative men recalled perceiving their mothers as less consistent. They also tended to see her as more tense. Nevertheless, they tended to be more assertive in her presence. Considering all items relating to the father (including those dealing with the men's perceptions of and feelings toward him, as well as their ratings of his success in various areas), the average score of the more creative men was significantly more positive on 17 out of 23 items than was true of the less creative men. With regard to the mother, the reverse was true. On 19 out of 23 items the average scores of the more creative men were significantly less positive.

Insofar as identification patterns are concerned, the two groups also differed. A significantly larger proportion of the more creative men wanted to be more like their fathers than their mothers in professional or occupational achievement and a similar trend was found with regard to moral characteristics.

From the minimal data presented, it is apparent that the more creative subjects grew up in home environments that differed from those of their less creative colleagues in interests and values. The two groups of subjects also differed in parent-child experiences. This is not the place to discuss the relevance of these factors to the problem of creativity (partly because not all the data have been presented, and partly because such a discussion would be beyond the scope of this monograph). Nevertheless, in such a presentation the possibility would be discussed that experiencing tension and inconsistency in the mother-child relationship may result in the child's having to use more of his own resources so that he can resolve the complexity he experiences. In so doing, his efforts are facilitated by identification with the father who emphasizes an area in which the child may fulfill his potentialities. Being successful in these experiences early in life, the developing child may then seek out the satisfaction of resolving complex issues in adult life.

The purpose in presenting the work of Roe and Stein, *et al.*, is to illustrate methods of understanding parent-child relationships that go further in seeking an understanding of the effects of early home life on future success than is possible with the social and demographic methods discussed in the previous section. When characteristics of parents are studied, when their social, professional, and educational characteristics are investigated, it is assumed that these have had differential effects on their children. But, these effects can occur only in parent-child transactions. Therefore, if the transactions are the important factors, why not investigate them directly?

Current psychological status

Over-all adjustment. To define "over-all adjustment" may be a difficult task for some, but apparently it posed no problem for the investigators in this area. For them over-all adjustment is defined in terms of test scores, which indicate that students fall within normal limits. Conversely, maladjustment is defined in terms of falling outside these limits.

The obvious assumption in the studies that follow is that the adjusted student will do well in college and that the poorly adjusted student will do less well. Presumably the latter has more problems, and to cope with them adequately requires energy that detracts from his capacity to utilize his potentiality and ability to do well in college. He may be unable to concentrate, to learn and to integrate course content, or else he may find himself uninterested in college. These are only some of the possibilities. No doubt there are others. Unfortunately, however, it is sometimes impossible to determine from the studies in this area the precise nature of the student's difficulties and therefore our understanding is limited. A second consequence is that one is unable, on the basis of the group data alone, to develop plans for helping students to overcome the problems they encounter. In any case, whatever the nature of the maladjustment, the assumption in several of the studies that follow is that adjustment is related to college success and maladjustment to lack of success, or failure. This is not to say that the academically successful student is without problems; in his case, however, what appears to be more important, as we shall see, is his attitude toward his problems.

Both projective and objective tests have been used to study over-all adjustment. In the main, however, results obtained with projective tests are neither as differentiating nor as consistent as those obtained with objective tests.

Using a sentence completion test, Berger and Sutker (1956) found over-all adjustment related to academic success. With the Rorschach Test, Thompson (1951) found similar results but Blechner and Carter (1956) found only low positive correlations. Cooper (1955), using the Rorschach Test with Munroe's scoring system, found significant correlations with grades for females over three semesters, and for males a significant relationship was found for only the third semester. Sopchak (1958), however, found that single Rorschach variables predict poorly as did Cronbach (1950) who also used the Munroe scoring system. The use of the "sign" technique with the Rorschach for predictive purposes has been appropriately criticized because it violates the Rorschach maxim that any single Rorschach sign is really meaningful only in the context of the total record (Cronbach, 1950).

Objective test measures of maturity or adjustment have yielded more consistent results and studies using such measures have indicated that the better adjusted student does do better academically.

Using the California Test of Mental Maturity, Barry and Jones (1959) found that 58 per cent of the probationary students had raw scores on the test that were lower than the lowest score made by any of the honor students. Approximately 29 per cent of the honor students had raw scores that were higher than the highest score achieved by a probationary student.

A more popular test for studying students' adjustment is the Minnesota Multiphasic Personality Inventory (MMPI). Stone and Ganung (1956) studied female students and used MMPI scores as independent variables to select two groups. One scored within the normal range and the other had T scores of 70 or higher on one or more of the clinical scales. The latter received significantly lower grade-point averages but the grades "could be described verbally only as a 'medium C' as compared to a 'high C'." A larger number of the "normal group" graduated, but there was no difference between the groups in number of quarters completed, although the trend was in the right direction. Hoyt and Norman (1954) also selected groups of maladjusted and normal freshmen in terms of MMPI scores. They hypothesized that the correlation between grades and ability should be lower for the maladjusted group than for students in the normal range. The hypothesis was confirmed when the Ohio State Psychological Examination was used as a measure of ability. But, it was not confirmed when the ACE was used as a measure of ability, possibly because the range on the ACE had been narrowed since it had been used in selection and admission procedures. The authors suggest the advisability of using separate regression equations for "normal" and "maladjusted" students.

High grades are associated with adjustment patterns at the freshman and senior levels. Moreover, seniors have better patterns of adjustment than freshmen, and freshmen who had both high grades and positive adjustment patterns continued to improve in adjustment patterns by the time they reached the senior year in college. These are the findings of Yeomans and Lundin (1957) who administered the MMPI to the top and bottom quarters of freshman and senior classes at Hamilton College. Poorer students in both classes were more maladjusted, particularly in the Psychopathic Deviate and Hypomania scales. They had more elevated scores on both scales. The authors say, "These students, in general, are probably more poorly motivated, irresponsible, and too active in other affairs to spend the necessary time and effort in their scholastic endeavors." In all traits measured except masculinity and depression, the freshman groups showed poorer adjustment than senior groups. The authors expected the freshmen to become better adjusted and thus continued their work in a follow-up study (Lundin and Kuhn, 1960) and found that students who were initially poorer in their freshman year did not show significant improvement in their MMPI scores over a four-year period. On the other hand, students who were originally in the top quarter of their freshman class did show definite improvement. "By the time the senior year is reached, the better students have become less worried about their personal health, less anxious, and more self-confident and reliable." And they conclude that, "Students who achieve better scholarship appear to be better adjusted in their college environment. The poorer students seem to be less responsible, react poorer to situations of stress, and are more concerned about their personal health."

College environments vary, consequently it need not always follow that seniors will be better adjusted than freshmen. In a study conducted at Vassar, Webster (1956) reports on the basis of MMPI data that "we were struck from the beginning by the proportionately large number of test profiles for freshmen in which there was little or no evidence of conscious disturbance, including depression and compulsion neurosis, but much evidence of rather complete and successful repression. It appears that the entering freshman is usually optimistic, compliant, friendly, and unlikely to complain much, either about personal difficulties or about the college situation. She is oriented toward adjustment and generally confident of achieving it." Among the seniors, however, Webster reports, "there has been some lifting of repression." On the MMPI they score higher on all scales except the Suppressor K scale. "The average senior is more willing and perhaps more able to admit her own weaknesses, or to describe such symptoms as she has." There is other evidence in the Vassar study that seniors have more neurotic complaints than freshmen. At Vassar this increase in neurotic symptoms over four years may have been stimulated by the college's standards and values. They may also reflect, as Sanford (1956) suggests, the growing pains that are attendant upon the greater educability of the students. While Webster's study provides no

data relating characteristics of freshmen or of seniors to academic success, it is nevertheless cited here to indicate that the hypothesis suggested by Lundin and Kuhn (1960) need not necessarily apply to all college situations.

Although maladjustment may limit academic success in some situations it should not be assumed that successful students are without problems (Kirk, 1955). MacLachlan and Burnett (1954) also found that, as freshmen, a group of "potentially superior" students had as wide a range of problems as did a group of "potentially not superior" students. Among the factors that differentiated the two groups was their attitude toward their problems. The potentially superior students tended to talk more easily and more enthusiastically about their plans, problems, and interests. It would appear then, that it is not only important to gather data on students' problems but also on the students' attitudes toward these problems.

Anxiety. Anxiety may have several sources, it may have a variety of manifestations, and when it is present it may serve as drive or it may be defended against in diverse ways and handicap the student in his achievement. A thorough study of the relationships between anxiety and college achievement would involve investigating all these factors. The available literature falls short of this goal. Nevertheless, occasionally data are presented that warrant further investigation.

One of the currently popular measures of anxiety is the Taylor Manifest Anxiety Scale (MAS) which contains items selected from the Minnesota Multiphasic Personality Inventory (MMPI). It has been used by itself or together with other measures as a predictor of college success and under both sets of conditions it generally proves to be inadequate as a predictor of college success.

When used by itself the MAS has correlated —.08 with grade-point average in the freshman year and in the same study the ACE correlated .51 with the criterion (Matarazzo, et al., 1954). This is consistent with the findings of Bendig and Klugh (1956) and Klugh and Bendig (1955) who report insignificant correlations between MAS and Quality Point Averages of students in an introductory psychology course.

The MAS has also been used in conjunction with other predictors but findings have not been replicated with the same tests so that definitive statements are not possible. Klugh and Bendig (1955) report that when the MAS is added to the ACE or Hr* scale separately it does not significantly increase the predictability of the criterion (Quality Point Averages of

---

*The Gough Hr (for honor point ratio) scale is part of the California Psychological Inventory (CPI) and yields data on personal values, beliefs, and self-definitions. Gough (1953) reports that in 11 cross-validation studies a mean correlation of .38 with grades in undergraduate psychology courses was obtained. In one study of extreme groups on the Hr scale it was found that the "highs" were seen by observers at the Institute of Personality Assessment and Research at Berkeley "as alert, clear-thinking, efficient, intelligent, pleasant, and resourceful." The "lows" were "seen as dull, immature, rebellious, rigid, and wary." On the basis of other information Gough claims that the Hr scale "is a predictor of academic achievement and not simply an indirect and inefficient measure of intellect."

students in an introductory psychology course). But, adding MAS to the ACE-Hr combination does result in a statistically significant increase in predictability over that obtained when the ACE and Hr scale are used without the MAS. Apparently when the ACE is left out of this combination similar results are not obtained (Bendig and Klugh, 1956). Possibly the MAS may act as a suppressor variable when used in conjunction with other predictors but more work has to be done in this regard that would involve item analyses of the MAS and the other tests used.

An attempt has also been made to relate the MAS to criteria other than grades. Bendig (1957) studied its relationships to *achievement level* and *achievement fluctuation*. Achievement level was defined as the student's grade in an introductory psychology course. This grade was based on a conversion system applied to the scores he obtained on four departmentally-constructed objective examinations. Achievement fluctuation was defined as the difference between each student's largest and smallest standard scores on the course examinations. The MAS scores were found not to be significantly related to either of these criteria.* Thus, grades of anxious students do not fluctuate more than do grades of nonanxious students nor does high anxiety as measured by the MAS handicap a student. Consequently, Bendig concludes that "The hypotheses that anxiety acts either as an increased goal-

---

*The Hr scale which was also used in this study yielded low but statistically significant correlations with achievement level but no significant relationship with achievement fluctuation.

oriented drive level in Ss or as a disrupter of goal-oriented behavior do not seem supported in this academic achievement situation."

One of the problems with the MAS may be that it is not clear what kind of anxiety it measures. Indeed, it is regarded as a measure of manifest anxiety that has been related to drive. But, a factor analysis of the test (O'Connor, *et al.*, 1956) suggests that it may be measuring at least five different types of anxiety. If this is so then it may be that the investigation of the relationship between a single score on the MAS and college success could obscure both theoretically and statistically significant findings that might be obtained if relationships between subscores on different types of anxiety measured and the criterion were studied. Along these lines it should be pointed out that investigators interested in the relationships between anxiety and college success need not be limited to the types of anxiety that are popular in the psychological test literature. For example, Piers and Singer (1953) indicate the value of differentiating between shame anxiety and guilt anxiety. Briefly, the former allows for growth or may be related to anxiety that serves as drives, while the latter may restrict or inhibit growth. Consequently, if appropriate test measures for these two types of anxiety were developed, it would be hypothesized that shame anxiety would be positively correlated and guilt anxiety would be negatively correlated with college success.

In contrast to others who have used anxiety in a rather global fashion, Sarason and Mandler (1952) have concentrated on a more specific kind of anxiety —test anxiety—and have presented results that are promising from both theoretical and practical standpoints. Sarason and Mandler theorized that anxiety is "a learned drive with the characteristics of a strong stimulus. When anxiety has been learned as a response to situations involving intellectual achievement (*e.g.*, test situations), two types of responses will tend to be evoked: (a) responses which are *not* task-relevant; self-centered feelings of inadequacy, attempts at leaving the situation, etc., and (b) task-relevant responses which reduce the anxiety by leading to completion of the task."

As a measure of anxiety they utilized a questionnaire that gathered information on students' attitudes and experiences in testing situations. The students were 492 sophomores and juniors at Yale University. On the basis of the students' distribution of scores on the questionnaire, four groups were established. One was a high anxiety group (HA_1) that represented cases going into the eighty-sixth percentile and one was a low anxiety group (LA_1) that represented cases going into the thirteenth percentile. The two other groups consisted of those students with scores that lie between the seventy-first and eighty-sixth percentiles (HA_2) and between the thirteenth and thirtieth percentiles (LA_2). The four groups could also be combined into two groups of high anxiety ($HA_1 + HA_2$) and low anxiety ($LA_1 + LA_2$).

For these students the following data were available: their scores on both scales of the Scholastic Aptitude Test (SAT), a predicted grade average (PGA), and an actual grade average (AGA).

Using these scores and grades as a basis for comparing the groups the authors assumed that the SAT scales would evoke task-irrelevant responses while actual grade averages (AGA, for the previous academic year) based on course examinations would evoke task-relevant responses. They reasoned that a course examination is not a novel situation. The student knows the examiner, he has some idea of what the examination will contain, and "there is time for previously learned anxiety-reducing task-relevant responses to become operative."

Therefore, they hypothesized that students with strong achievement and anxiety drive should do less well on the SAT scales and have lower predicted grade averages (which are based in part on the SAT as well as other factors such as high school grades) than students with high anxiety. These variables would be effected by task-irrelevant responses. It was also hypothesized, however, that the opposite relationship would obtain with actual grade averages. High anxiety students would have higher grades because examinations evoked task-relevant responses.

As a first test of this hypothesis the data for the two extreme anxiety groups (HA_1 vs. LA_1) were analyzed and the results were in the predicted direction: "the HA_1 group obtained significantly lower SAT scores, a significantly lower PGA, and a higher AGA which approaches significance."

However, it will be recalled that four anxiety groups were established. Sarason and Mandler therefore investigated whether the relationships obtained for the extreme groups would also obtain among several of the other possible combinations. Here analysis of the data revealed that there were no significant relationships between anxiety and the dependent variables if one compared the two groups of students who were high on anxiety (HA_1 vs. HA_2). Furthermore, there were also no significant relationships obtained for the two middle groups (HA_2 vs. LA_2). However, when the data obtained for the two groups of subjects at the low end of the anxiety continuum (LA_1 vs. LA_2) were analyzed, "the results are all in the expected direction: the LA_1 group obtained significantly higher SAT scores, a significantly higher PGA, and lower AGA which is not significant but in the expected direction."

On the basis of these results as well as other data on the intercorrelations among the dependent variables for each of the anxiety subgroups, Sarason and Mandler argue that, as measured by their questionnaire, "the low end of the anxiety distribution approximates a behavioral continuum while the high end does not." In explaining their results these investigators suggest that the two groups of subjects at the high end of the anxiety continuum may "differ not in strength of their anxiety responses but in the ways in which they defend themselves against recognition and expression of such responses." Thus, there are likely to be differences in learned defense mechanisms between the two groups. The authors also suggest the possibility that among the low anxiety students defense mechanisms are not as likely to be evoked but for them, too, "The possibility cannot be overlooked . . . that in some cases a low anxiety score might also be related to the need for defense."

The theorizing as well as the thorough analysis of data by Sarason and Mandler indicate how complex the relationships between anxiety and success in college might be. There are no simple and sovereign solutions to the problem which can replace the effort necessary to explore these relationships more fully than has been the case heretofore.

Control and compulsiveness. Excessive control and rigidity may block the student's openness to new experiences as well as his capacity to integrate new experiences. Consequently, it may well be expected, and indeed the major theme of the studies in this section is, that personality characteristics from which one might infer the strong need for control, if not rigidity, are related to poor college achievement. But these studies do more than that, they also illustrate the importance of specifying the factors that make up the criterion and provide some clues, regarding the interaction between interest tests and personality factors.

Stern, Stein, and Bloom (1956), using an approach about which we shall have more to say later (p. 50), sought to synthesize purely hypothetical personality syndromes that would have predictable consequences for interaction in specified situations. Using Stern's Inventory of Beliefs, it was possible to differentiate three major personality types — Stereopaths (S's), Non-Stereopaths (N's), and Rationals (R's).

The Stereopath is "a hypothetical individual who may be characterized in terms of depersonalized and codified social relationships, pervasive acceptance of authority as absolute, inhibition and denial of impulses, and rigid orderliness and conformity in behavior."

The Non-Stereopath is characterized "by highly personalized and individualized social relationships, pervasive rejection of authority figures, spontaneous and acceptant impulse life, and nonconforming flexibility in behavior."

Finally, the Rational individual, in terms of this system, is one "whose social relationships are distant and impersonal, cathecting ideas rather than persons."

For our purposes, we shall limit ourselves to the findings on the S's (Stereopaths) and the N's (Non-Stereopaths) since they might be regarded as differing most from each other on such global characteristics as control and rigidity.

A variety of results are reported by Stern, Stein, and Bloom (1956) concerning the placement test results and learning outcomes for groups of S's and N's of different sizes in a general education program in a midwestern college. On the placement tests the N's scored significantly higher in the humanities, social sciences, English, and a test in language that concerned itself with the analysis of language as a symbolic system. These results were consistent with inferences about lack of verbal facility, flexibility, and skill in analysis that would be associated with the stereopathic syndrome.

At the time of entering college, the N's and S's also differed in their vocational preferences. Over two-thirds of the Stereopaths expressed an interest in instrumental activities (accounting, engineering, business, law, and medicine), while more than two-thirds of the Non-Stereopaths expressed interests in consummatory pursuits of both an interpersonal and expressive nature (psychology, sociology, teaching, music, art, and literature).

While in college, the Stereopaths and Non-Stereopaths also differed in their classroom behavior. Data were collected on covert classroom behavior as revealed by the method of stimulated recall. This aspect of the investigation was based on only 20 subjects. Nevertheless, several rather interesting trends appeared. The "data indicate the Stereopath students to be somewhat more active participants in the classroom process, as reflected by the frequency of thoughts involving evaluation of the class process. Thus, they are more frequently involved in considerations of the relevance, accuracy, or meaningfulness of some class activity. The object of these evaluations most often involves another student in the class, however, and their tone is largely negative in character, involving either direct expression (covert) of discomfort, pain, tension, and annoyance, or at best, ambivalence. In contrast, the N's tend to participate passively, simply following or listening to the idea under consideration. Furthermore, their thoughts are oriented in terms of the present, whereas the Stereopaths are reflecting more commonly upon past events."

A third source of data came from instructors' ratings of the students on five scales: (1) open-mindedness, (2) emotional adjustment, (3) extent of classroom participation, (4) type of classroom participation, and (5) academic potential. The average ratings for the Non-Stereopath students were higher than those obtained by the Stereopaths. The authors suggest that the relationship between the over-all rating on the five previously mentioned variables and the score on the Inventory of Beliefs stemmed largely from the fifth scale which was regarded as a measure of the identification between instructor and student.

The data on the students' classroom behavior and the instructors' higher ratings for Non-Stereopath students are obviously related and consistent with goals and value systems of the faculty and the university in which the study was conducted. Stern, Stein, and Bloom say, "These data suggest, on the one hand, that the Stereopath is engaged in covert behavior in the classroom which is predominantly critical and hostile, and on the other hand, that the instructors are inclined to respond less favorably to these students than they do toward the N's. This is a further reflection of the essentially nonsupportive atmosphere of the college towards S-type students. Both the scholastic and social environment of this institution are in large measure opposed to the rigidity, conventionality, dependence, and general orientation of the presumed Stereopath individual. Furthermore, the college's high scholastic standards require that a student be able to draw freely upon all of his abilities. To the extent that the effective energy of the Stereopath may be assumed to be still further reduced by the degree of anxiety and repression characterizing representatives of the syndrome, it seems likely that such students encounter much greater difficulty in their adjustment to the college program during the first year than is true of the N's."

There are additional differences between Stereopath and Non-Stereopath students. For example, a significantly larger proportion of Stereopaths were making a poorer adjustment to college as indicated by the students' advisers' comments than was true of the Non-Stereopaths. However, of those students who gave evidence of emotional disturbance, a significantly larger proportion of Non-Stereopaths sought help than was true of the Stereopaths. Also, a significantly larger proportion of Stereopaths were found to have withdrawn from the college (and most of the withdrawals occurred at the end of the first semester) even when both N's and S's are matched for scores on the ACE.

Few of the Stereopath students gave explicit reasons for leaving college; their records, however, suggest that they were disappointed in the number of courses they had to take. "In general, these students seem to have more ambition than capacity, although their most serious limitation is due to the autistic nature of their goals rather than to intellectual deficiency."

Kim (1958) reports a study which is consistent with the above results, although a different criterion was used. In this study, 25 pairs of Stereopaths and 25 pairs of Non-Stereopaths were compared in terms of honor point ratios and it was found that the latter had the higher grades.

Non-Stereopaths do not do better, however, in all situations and with all criteria. It is not always true that a faculty will prefer behavior that characterizes Non-Stereopath students, as we found in the study reported by Stern, Stein, and Bloom (1956). Kelly (1958) reports a study where a faculty appears to prefer Stereopath students. He selected three groups of students for his research. One group received instructor grades that were generally higher than their term-end examinations. The second group consisted of students whose term-end examination grades were higher than instructor grades, and in the third group instructor grades and term-end examination grades were about the same. Using the Stern Inventory of Beliefs, it was found that higher instructor groups were more compulsive, conforming, rigid, and generally insecure than their opposites.

The two studies of Stereopaths and Non-Stereopaths just reviewed indicate that the relationship between stereopathy and a criterion of college success is a function of the factors that make up the criterion. (Or, as we shall see later in discussing the *Transactional Approach*, p. 50, it is critical to differentiate between a criterion and a standard of performance.) Where the faculty or the college environment values autonomous behavior for the student and where the criterion of college success reflects the student's capacity to use freely his own resources, then the Non-Stereopath student does better. On the other hand, in those situations in which it is necessary that a student submerge his own individuality for him to be successful, then the student who is inclined to be stereopathic in his orientation is likely to be more successful.

There are other approaches to studying the relationships between control and compulsiveness and college success. One of the more interesting ones is a study by Frederiksen and Melville (1954). This study also indicates the need for further information on the predictability of certain groups of students and it highlights the importance of the interaction between technique and students for purposes of prediction. In other words, it indicates the potential value of developing separate predictive measures for different subgroups of students, or of including among the predictors various scores representing membership in certain types of student groups.

Frederiksen and Melville (1954) started with the observation that some students study hard at courses they like and neglect those they do not. Other students, however, do not differentiate between courses and study all courses equally hard. Consequently, with compulsiveness defined here "as a tendency to be thorough and perfectionistic in one's work without regard for the amount of intrinsic enjoyment of the work itself," the authors hypothesized that noncompulsiveness and compulsiveness would be important ways of establishing subgroups of students and that the correlation between grades and interest measures would be different for the two groups. The subjects were students who completed their first year in the School of Engineering at Princeton University and the criterion was first-year average grades in engineering. The Accountant scale of the Strong Vocational Interest Blank and the Cooperative Reading Comprehension Test were used to differentiate between compulsive and noncompulsive students. Students who scored above the average of the group on the Accountant scale were "compulsives" as were

those who read slowly in relation to ability (as measured by the regression of Speed of Comprehension on the Vocabulary score). The scores on the Strong VIB (other than Accountant scale) were then correlated with the criterion and "the agreement of the data with the hypothesis is, in general, greater than would be expected by chance . . . that noncompulsive students . . . are somewhat more predictable than compulsive students on the basis of interest scores." The differences between the groups are not due to consistent differences in variability between groups.

This study was replicated by Frederiksen and Gilbert (1960) and the result previously reported "seems to hold up only for the occupational keys most logically related to engineering—Mathematician, Physicist, Engineer, and Chemist—when the groups are defined on the basis of reading speed relative to vocabulary."

Why should interest measures correlate more highly for the noncompulsive than for the compulsive student? If one assumes that the interest measures are valid, then one may conclude that if the individual had his own way he would pursue these interests. The compulsive student is not so free. There are factors which impel him to deny his own interests or hold them in abeyance to satisfy other needs (for example, to show that he is "good" or "excellent" in all areas or because his instructors, as Kelly's study suggests, reward it). Therefore, interest measures alone are not very predictable for him since they are overridden by motivational factors. The noncompulsive student is not beset with these overriding factors. He can more easily and more directly fulfill his interests and therefore, for him, interest scores are more effective predictors.

Need achievement. The need to work for and attain goals, need achievement, is a motivational factor that one would expect to be associated with success in the academic environment as it has been related to achievements in other areas (McClelland, 1953, 1961). To obtain data on this need, investigators have utilized three major techniques: paper and pencil tests (primarily the *Edwards' Personal Preference Schedule* (1954), projective tests (usually TAT or TAT-like pictures which are often scored following McClelland), and indices of level of aspiration.

In general, need achievement measures correlate positively with grades, either when they are used as the sole predictors or when they are used in conjunction with other predictors. There are, however, variations in how effectively different methods for measuring need achievement provide data that result in these positive correlations.

Bendig (1958) found the need achievement score on the Edwards' Scale to be a better predictor of self-reported quality point average than a vocabulary test and the Hr scale of Gough's test in a study of 164 male students enrolled in six daytime sections of an introductory psychology course. Both second semester freshmen and seniors were included in this study and three predictor variables were used: (a) vocabulary—consisting of 20 relatively difficult five-choice synonym items from the Cooperative Vocabulary Test, (b) the 32-item Hr scale which is designed to measure temperament characteristics of high achieving college students, and (c) the need achievement scale of the Edwards' test. The correlation between need achievement and self-reported quality point average was low (.23) but higher than that obtained with the other tests. A combination of need achievement and vocabulary correlated .29 with the criterion and was significantly higher than the correlation obtained for need achievement alone. However, adding the Hr scale to need achievement, to vocabulary, or to the vocabulary-need achievement combination did not significantly increase the predictability of the criterion.

The Edwards' measure of need achievement also correlated higher with grade-point average (.42) than an achievement score based on six of McClelland's TAT-like pictures (.34) but then neither correlated as well with the criterion as an academic aptitude test (.55). The academic aptitude tests plus the McClelland score correlated .63 with the criterion and the aptitude test plus the Edwards correlated .64 with the criterion, while all three combined correlated .68 with grade-point average (Weiss, *et al.,* 1959).

Pictures selected from Murray's TAT series (Murray, 1943) have also been used, generally in conjunction with other measures, to obtain data on need achievement. Morgan (1952) used the TAT as well as some structured questions to investigate the achievement motivation of 136 male sophomores at the University of Minnesota. ACE scores and honor point ratios were available for all students and they were divided into three categories according to scholastic achievement. Achievers had honor grades, while nonachievers obtained grades around the freshman mean. The results indicated that the achievers scored significantly higher on need achievement than did the nonachievers. Using semistructured questions (for example, "Who are you?"; "If you could be granted any three wishes what might you wish?"); the author also found the same result.

The results obtained by Morgan were not replicated by Parrish and Rethlingshafer (1954) possibly because, among other factors, the latter used a more homogeneous population of high intellectual capacity.

Parrish and Rethlingshafer studied two groups of 24 males that consisted of both first and second-year students. All of the students scored above the ninetieth percentile on the American Council on Education Psychological Examination (ACE) and as groups they were similar on age, geographical origin, marital status, educational history, continuity of school attendance, and parental education. The only background information on which they differed was number of interests. Thus they were quite homogeneous. What did distinguish the two groups were their grade averages. One group had a grade average of below C and the other group had a grade average between A and B. To gather data on achievement motivation two of the TAT pictures plus two other pictures that would presumably tap need achievement were used. The stories were scored in three different ways: by McClelland's method (1949), by one scorer who tried to classify the stories into groups using all possible

cues whether related to achievement or not, and by several scorers who suggested ideas as to factors that might be related on rational grounds to need achievement. None of these three different techniques provided data that differentiated significantly between the two groups of students.

Other projective techniques in addition to the TAT have been used to gather achievement data. Chahbazi (1956) studied the relationships between several predictor variables and grade-point average. The predictor variables included: secondary school averages, cooperative reading test, cooperative science test, Cornell Mathematics Test, Ohio State University Psychological Test, and the Cornell Orientation Inventory. The multiple correlation between the six predictor variables and the criterion was .512. Two projective tests were then added to the predictor variables—a Picture Stimuli Test and a Sound Stimuli Test. The Picture Stimuli Test was that of a musician, and the sound test was a recording of a symphony. Need achievement was scored following McClelland (1949). When the projective predictors were added to the previous six, the correlation was raised from .512 to .633. The six predictors accounted for 26 per cent of the variance while all eight predictors accounted for 40 per cent of the variance.

Still other measures have been used to study achievement motivation. Nix (1960), using an "Index of Study and Work Habits" that included a measure of achievement, found that it and a self-ideal score made considerable contributions to the regression of scores in several curricular areas. In other instances, achievement motivation has been approached through measures of the student's level of aspiration. Schultz and Ricciuti (1954) studied goal discrepancy scores for several groups of college students. These scores were derived from aspiration statements made in two experimental tests and regular course examinations. Little, if any, correlation was found to exist between goal discrepancy scores and previous college achievement.

Worrell (1959), however, followed a different approach to the level of aspiration problem that yielded some rather interesting data. His approach differed from that used by others in that he utilized discrepancy scores based on a student's estimates of his performance rather than his actual performance. Then too, he viewed discrepancy scores as reflecting a dimension of reality-unreality. For him the reality-unreality dimension was "defined as any discrepancy between estimated performance or effort and some other aspiration estimate. The larger a discrepancy the more an individual may be regarded as unrealistic." Consequently, he hypothesized "that persons with highly discrepant scores base their estimates of performance on unrealistic considerations of a wishful or avoidant nature. Such individuals, when faced with academic performance situations, are expected to invoke more unrealistic and avoidant responses than subjects with lower discrepancy scores. Thus, for example, of two persons with identical estimates of previous performance but divergent estimates of subsequent performance, the one with the more discrepant score is expected to perform more poorly

since achievement situations for him evoke more unrealistic behaviors."

As his subjects, Worrell studied 421 students (almost the entire student body) who attended a small liberal arts college that seeks to encourage a desire for learning rather than for achieving grades. In keeping with this goal, grades in this college are not revealed to the students by their instructors although grades are assigned for administrative purposes. At the end of each year, however, the student is given a relative decile standing in his class. This information is available to the advanced students in the study but not to the freshmen since they had not, at the time of the study, completed their first year. The attitude of the college toward grades and the type of information the students had about their grades are relevant since they might have increased the probability of reality distortion.

To gather information on level of aspiration and discrepancy scores Worrell again deviated from other level of aspiration studies in that he did not utilize artificial tasks but rather questions which involved "estimates that were highly related to the type of performance which we wished to predict." The questions he used were:

"1. How hard do you work on your studies relative to other students?

2. How do you think your average grade compares with those of your classmates?

3. If you plan to return next year, how well do you expect to do in comparison with other members of your class?

4. If you really tried to do well and worked near the limits of your capacity, how would your average grades compare with those of your classmates?

5. How well would you like to do in order to be reasonably well satisfied according to your own standards?"

Using these questions, Worrell tested the following specific hypotheses: "Academic adjustment is inversely related to the degree to which students' estimates of (a) what their performance would be when working near the limits of their capacity exceed their estimates of how hard they have worked in the past; (b) their future performance are above their estimates of previous performance; (c) what their performance would be when working near the limits of capacity are above their estimates of previous performance; (d) what they would be reasonably satisfied with in their performance exceed their estimates of previous performance."

Thus, it was possible to obtain four different discrepancy scores which could be used as four different predictors.

A study of the relationships between aspiration discrepancy scores and both decile ranks and total grade averages (the criteria) for freshmen, sophomores, juniors, and seniors yielded statistically significant findings in all comparisons except one (the relationship between effort, as suggested by the first hypothesis, and the decile rank for seniors). On the basis of these results Worrell concludes, "that the student who behaves unrealistically, or more specifically, the one who perceives his reasonable level of performance satisfaction as lying above previous achievement, has aspirations markedly beyond past performance, estimates his potential capacity for performance as lying far above the effort he expends, and believes that he can achieve far beyond what he already has by pressing himself to the limit of his ability, will tend to attain and continue to attain a lower scholastic standing. On the other hand, the student who holds moderate aspirations, perceives his effort as being commensurate with his potential capacity for performance, does not see his performance as markedly improving by making a 'total push,' and whose standards of acceptable satisfaction are below his previous achievement, tends to obtain grade success."

Since Worrell had other data for his subjects, he was also able to compare the correlations between his level of aspiration measures and the criteria with those obtained by other predictors. For all students he had high school achievement measures and ability measures. A comparison between the predictive capacity of the level of aspiration measures and the criteria and those obtained by the ability and high school achievement measures indicated that a multiple correlation based on the four aspiration measures was higher than that obtained by a multiple correlation based on the other two measures. The highest multiple correlations, however, were obtained by using all six measures. Furthermore, when the four aspiration measures were combined into a single index it was possible to differentiate between graduates and nongraduates for freshmen and sophomores. The discriminative power of the index was reduced for juniors. Finally, the same index did not differentiate among graduates and nongraduates among below C students but it did make this differentiation among the C and above C students.

In summarizing the studies reviewed on the relationships between achievement motivation and college success, we find that a variety of techniques have been used in this area and by and large they indicate that whether used as a sole predictor or in combination with other predictors need achievement is positively correlated with criteria of college success. However, one needs to be certain that the need is appropriate to the task.

Masculinity-femininity. Psychologically, what we mean when we say that an individual has a "high feminine component" is that he may be expected to be high on sensitivity, awareness of feelings, artistic and cultural interests, receptive attitude, and so forth. On the other hand, when we say that an individual has a "high masculine component" what we mean is that he may be expected to be an individual with a capacity for action, assertiveness, orientation toward external objects, and so forth. Theoretically, the well-integrated individual is capable of the attitudes and behaviors reflected in both masculine and feminine components. At different times the individual is capable of being aware of his own feelings or attending to external objects, of being receptive or assertive, and so forth. It is therefore unfortunate that studies exploring the relationships between masculinity and femininity and college success usually regard masculinity-femininity as a single psychological continuum. The obtained results, however, are, in a sense, consistent with theory, for the data indicate that the predictive efficiency of masculinity-femininity scores are contingent on the sex of the student. Male students who score high on femininity are more successful in college than those males who score low, while among female students a high masculine score is more critical for college success.

Drake (1956) found that MMPI profiles of male counselees who were judged to be lacking in academic motivation by their counselors could be differentiated from the MMPI profiles of other counselees. Their profiles could be distinguished by the following pattern: the Schizophrenia (Sc) and the Mania (Ma) scales were paired among the three highest coded scales and the Social Introversion (Si) scale was coded among the two lowest scales. Drake also found that those students who were judged as lacking in academic motivation did not score high on the Mf scale. This led to the suggestion (Drake and Oetting, 1957) that where the nonmotivated pattern (Ma-Sc paired high with Si low) was obtained counselors might well check the possibility that a student's difficulties may be due to the fact that he lacks academic motivation. On the other hand, if the nonmotivated pattern occurred in conjunction with a high Mf score then the hypothesis might have to be modified since there are indications that the Mf scale "is in some manner associated with the ability to adjust socially and personally to situations where other MMPI patterns indicate difficulties." In other words, the Mf scale might act as a suppressor variable when associated with certain MMPI patterns.

With these considerations in mind, Drake and Oetting (1957) undertook a study in which they predicted that: (1) Beginning freshmen who had the nonmotivated profile and who did not have the Mf scale coded high would obtain lower grades during their first semester in college than the total group of their fellow freshmen. (2) Beginning freshmen who had the nonmotivated pattern but who had Mf scale scores that were coded high would *not* obtain lower grades than the total freshman group. The results of the study confirmed the predictions. The non-motivated low Mf group did obtain significantly lower grade-point averages than the total group as well as their counterparts who had high Mf scores. Moreover, insofar as the nonmotivated high Mf group was concerned they not only exceeded the non-motivated low Mf group, but their grades also exceeded those of the total group of students.

An additional finding of the Drake and Oetting study was that in a subsample, Mf scores, used either alone or in conjunction with an intellectual predictor, did not contribute very much to the prediction of grades at the end of the first semester. For this subsample Mf scores alone correlated only $+.17$ with grades and in conjunction with the ACE the multiple correlation was raised to $+.47$. However, the ACE alone correlated $+.46$ with grades.

In view of their findings which indicate that the Mf score of the MMPI serves better for predictive purposes when the population of students is homogeneous in certain respects than when it is not, Drake and Oetting suggest, "It appears that, although the scores on a single personality scale may be related to some underlying construct, factorial or otherwise, the determination of behavior is unlikely to depend on a variable simple enough to be measured by a single scale. In order to predict behavior for a group, the group must be relatively homogeneous for the behavior. Consequently, the group must be selected on the basis of as many underlying traits as possible."

Yeomans and Lundin (1957) studied the top and bottom quarters of freshman and senior classes and found that those in the top quarter of both classes scored significantly higher on the Mf scale of the MMPI than did men in the general population. Lundin and Kuhn (1960) followed these same students over a four-year period and found that there was a strong tendency for feminine interests to increase over this period and most particularly for the better students.

Insofar as female students are concerned, Brown (1960) found that students who were regarded as "potentially superior" scored higher on masculinity as measured by the Mellon scale than those who were not regarded as "potentially superior."

The studies reviewed thus far on the relationship between masculinity-femininity and college success have utilized rather simple techniques to gather their data and they have involved relatively little theorizing. The study by Webster (1956) that follows is cited, in spite of the fact that it does not relate masculinity-femininity to some measure of college success, because of its sophisticated theorizing and utilization of several techniques to illuminate the complexities of the relationships that may be found in this area.

The study by Webster was conducted at Vassar and both verbal and nonverbal tests of masculinity-femininity were used. Among the verbal tests were:

"MF I (Conventionality)—Preference for conventionally feminine roles and interests.

"MF II (Passivity) — Lack of aggressiveness, of dominance, of manipulativeness, docility, modesty, moral sensitivity.

"MF III (Feminine Sensitivity) — Emotionality, fantasy, introspection, 'neurotic trends,' and aesthetic interests." This scale was lengthened by adding highly correlating non-Mf items including a large number of neurotic symptoms.

Using these tests, Webster found that seniors at Vassar score slightly lower on the first two scales and slightly higher on the third than freshmen. Webster therefore suggests "that seniors tend to become more 'masculine' in the sense of being less conventional and less passive, but at the same time more 'feminine' in their inner life...."

Sanford (1956) in commenting on these findings makes the following interesting point. "Being less 'feminine,' " he says, "is closely related to being more educated and more mature. Increasing acceptance of intellectual values, decreasing stereotypy in the perception of the sexes and of sex roles, increasing differentiation in the conception of what one can do without endangering one's feminine identity are bound to make for lower scores on the traditional femininity scales. It is interesting to note, however, that 'feminine sensitivity,' which may well have sources in physiology and in early identifications, does not decrease during the four years; 'feminine' interests and feminine role behavior, that is, conventionality and passivity, can be understood as later and more superficial acquisitions, and, hence, more susceptible to decrease as the individual becomes more mature and more educated."

The Vassar study also included a rather interesting exploration in the use of nonverbal Mf tests. Two such tests were used, one of figure completions, the Franck Drawing Completion Test (Franck and Rosen, 1949) and one of figure preferences, the Barron-Welsh Figure Preference Test (1953). In large samples of freshmen, it was found that, "those who complete drawings in ways more characteristic of women exhibit a slight tendency to say that they prefer, or 'like,' figures, or drawings, which have masculine symbolism, and those whose drawing completions are masculine tend to prefer feminine figures; the relationship is attenuated by a number of factors having to do with the theory of object choice. For example, girls with strong conscious preferences for the father (rather than the mother) are known not only to complete drawings in masculine ways but also to like those figures which are masculine; they also score lower on verbal femininity factors and higher on scales measuring rebelliousness.

"Freshmen who complete drawings in ways characteristic of men and who prefer the figures with feminine characteristics are less flexible, more authoritarian, and more repressed (especially in the area of erotic interest in men) than are other students. Conventionally feminine students, that is, those whose drawing completions are feminine, but whose object choices (figure preferences) are masculine, are found to score higher than other students on verbal femininity scales. Narcissistic students, or those whose drawing completions and figure preferences both are feminine, score lowest when compared with other students on the CPI Social Responsibility scale and highest on a narcissism scale based on verbal self-description. It should be emphasized, however, that most of the differences just described are not large, and that they were easily discernible only in extreme groups. It seems likely that the student who is *not* extreme on these measures of preference for kinds of figure drawings is using a mixture of two attitudes, one a narcissistic attitude in which she 'chooses herself,' the other a complementary attitude in which she chooses something she conceives to be different from herself."

Although, as Webster says, the differences "are not large," it is likely the approach used in the Vassar study, which includes a combination of techniques plus theory, may well lead to a better understanding of the relationships between masculinity and femininity and academic success than other approaches.

Typologies. The studies reviewed thus far concerned themselves, in general, with single personality variables (for example, need achievement) or with some global personality characteristic (for example, maladjustment). These variables have been related to a criterion of college success either by themselves or in conjunction with other predictors. Another approach that has been used is one in which samples of students are selected in terms of certain homogeneous characteristics and then specific psychological variables are used for differential predictions for each of the homogeneous samples. An example of this approach was presented above in the work of Drake and Oetting (1957) on the predictive value of high and low Mf scores for nonmotivated students. When such homogeneous groups are established on the basis of meaningful constellations or clusters of personality characteristics and when the total constellation is utilized in the sense of a single variable then the investigator is using a typological analysis of psychological variables. In other words, typologies are means of representing groups of individuals in terms of homogeneous characteristics. When used to predict college success a prediction is made for the typology.

To arrive at the typologies that may exist in one's population of subjects one might use a typological system developed by other investigators or one might use appropriate statistical techniques to analyze one's own data in an effort to determine the types that exist in one's own population. Examples of both approaches are presented below.

McArthur and King (1954) utilized Vorhaus' (1952) typological system for dealing with Rorschach Test data. Vorhaus distinguished four Rorschach Test patterns: Type I — the merely formal record; Type II — the animal-movement dominated record; Type III — the human-movement dominated record; Type IV—the record in which inanimate and color responses dominate. Using these types, Mc-

Arthur and King inquired into the frequency with which the Vorhaus types occurred in Rorschach records of students referred to Harvard's Department of Hygiene for academic or personal reasons and compared these data with the frequencies with which these types appeared in the records of a control group. Analysis of the data revealed that Types I, II, and III were comparatively rare in both the experimental and control groups and did not differentiate between the two populations. Type IV records, however, were more frequent and occurred significantly more frequently (at the .01 level) among the students referred to the Department of Hygiene. McArthur and King point out that students who present such records "are usually in academic trouble as a matter of administrative fact or else are 'failing' in their own eyes because they have not met their own and their parents' level of aspiration." Vorhaus presents additional information on the psychodynamics of this type and some of the factors involved in its developmental history which helps explain why students of this type should be referred for help. She says, "... the subject (of this type) is responsive to affective stimulation; indeed, he is responsive to a point where moments of strong feeling occur as often, or almost as often, as those when a more surface pleasantness is all that is evoked. ... The subject may have succeeded in repressing recognition that this is so." In their developmental histories one finds "... the 'good' home, the submissive child, and the awareness of pressure. ... Since the resentment (of the pressure) cannot be overcome, the psychological need becomes that of

preventing it from being experienced as associated with the environment. This is done by turning the hostility against the self for the 'guilt' of harboring the resentment. ... With this accomplished, the subject is able to feel that 'Mother and Father are entirely just in all their demands and expectations. It is I who am guilty for not cooperating with them. It is because of my inadequacy and inferiority that their "good" plans have not worked out'."

McArthur and King also investigated further their Type III records and after altering Vorhaus' criteria somewhat they established a Type IIIb which occurred more frequently in their control than in their experimental group. A student with this type of Rorschach record they describe as one who not only has ability to relate himself "to the environment, but (has) specific skill at tying ... (his) impulses in with the social environment."

Thus, McArthur and King were able to find two types of students, one that was more likely to be referred for problems and the other that was less likely to be referred for problems. Moreover, in determining these types they also had simultaneously a fair amount of information about their psychodynamics which helped explain why the types were more frequently represented in each of the two groups. As with all other researches that use typological systems in this area, McArthur and King did not determine all the types in their experimental or control groups, but rather concentrated on the frequency with which certain discernible types appeared in their populations. We shall return to this problem later.

A second approach to typologies is not to utilize available typological systems but to develop one's own on the basis of statistical analysis of a test battery or questionnaire. Previously (p. 28) a study was presented (Stern, Stein, and Bloom, 1956) in which the Inventory of Beliefs was analyzed to pick out students who could be classified as Stereopaths, Non-Stereopaths, and Rationals. Middleton and Guthrie (1959) also used a technique of statistical analysis for arriving at their types but their research illustrates another important methodological point that is of value for researches that seek to determine the relationships between personality factors and college success.

Middleton and Guthrie followed up a suggestion made by Stern, Stein, and Bloom (1956) that the same criterion of college success may be achieved in a variety of ways by a variety of personality types. On the theoretical level this suggestion was consistent with the principle of equipotentiality and on the practical level this suggestion was made to counteract the impression that might be gained from some prediction studies that there was only a pattern of psychological variables that might significantly relate to a criterion. To determine their personality types, Middleton and Guthrie used transposed factor analysis with the responses of two groups of business management students to a 300-item personality questionnaire drawn from Murray's (1938) work. With this analysis they established several factors for high achieving and low achieving students. The students were 14 business management students who had attained at least junior standing and with grade averages of 2.50 or higher (A = 4.00). These were compared with a group of 14 students whose grade averages were below 2.00. Both groups had done equally well in high school. The high group, however, had scored significantly higher on a test of college aptitude. Five factors of persons were found for high students and four factors were found for low students.

The five factors for high achieving students (10 of the 14 students had factor loadings of at least .40 on one or more of the factors) were:

"Factor H-I. This factor correlates positively with nurturance and dominance and negatively with abasement, succorance, and narcissism. Achievement to these Ss appears to mean power and approval.

"Factor H-II. Autonomy, aggression, counteraction, and achievement correlate positively, while abasement and affiliation are negatively correlated. Achievement for this group seems to be an expression of resentment and independence.

"Factor H-III. The needs for succorance, exhibition, abasement, sentience, and affiliation are all correlated positively with this factor. In contrast to the preceding factor, this factor presents strong dependence.

"Factor H-IV. Deference, nurturance, infavoidance or avoidance of failure, extraception, and dominance correlated positively with Factor H-IV. These Ss appear to be pursuing goals of social prestige and influence. Achievement may be an avenue whereby they can be thought well of.

"Factor H-V. Aggression shows a low positive correlation, while high negative correlations appear with nurturance, affiliation, deference, infavoidance, and understanding. Achievement appears to be related to a hostile aggressive denial of tender socialized feelings."

The four factors for the low achievers (11 of the 14 students had factor loadings of at least .40 on one or more of the factors) were:

"Factor L-I. The following needs showed high correlations with this factor: sentience, succorance, infavoidance, narcissism, and abasement, while counteraction or a need to overcome defeat was highly negatively correlated. These Ss appear to be preoccupied with pleasures.

"Factor L-II. Nurturance, understanding, extraception and affiliation are positively correlated with this need, while succorance, abasement, rejection, and infavoidance are denied. These persons appear to be consistently extroverted in their relationships.

"Factor L-III. Extraception is the only positively correlated need, while sentience, autonomy, narcissism, exhibitionism, and succorance are negatively related to this factor. This group seems intent on disavowing social shortcomings.

"Factor L-IV. Needs of exhibition, dominance, understanding, and affiliation are positively related to this factor, while the S seeks to avoid blame and threats to his self-esteem. These Ss appear to be preoccupied with power and acceptance."

These factors of persons or typologies are promising but they do require additional confirmation.

Compared to other kinds of studies, the number in which typologies have been used in the prediction of college success is small. It is likely, however, that more of these will be carried out in the future. Their increase will be encouraged by the use of available computers that make it possible to carry out the statistical analyses with comparative ease. Typologies are also consistent with the principle of equipotentiality. There is no one complex of personality characteristics that is uniquely related to currently available criteria of college success. There are several pathways to a goal and the goal may differ in psychological significance for different types of individuals. These phenomena are not adequately treated when single psychological variables are used in predictive studies.

Although typologies are potentially quite significant in furthering our understanding of students and in increasing the accuracy of our predictions it is possible that their development and use may have to contend with certain obstacles.

At the present time no study seeking to relate types of students to some criterion of college success can classify each of the students studied into a type. Some students can be typed while others cannot. The problem does not reside within the concept of typology but rather confronts the entire field of personality research. The field of personality, let alone other areas in psychology, does not yet possess an agreed upon system of variables for the development of a classification system that may be used with all individuals. And, in passing, it should be indicated that no science has made much progress without such a system. Consequently, the use of typologies in the prediction of college success may well be limited until psychologists combine their efforts to develop an agreed upon set of variables for the study of individuals.

Another possible obstacle confronting the use of typologies is of a different character. Typologies may be looked upon with disfavor because it may be feared that their use may tend to stereotype individuals. It may also be feared that they may achieve the same status as typologies concerned with measuring physical characteristics where it was assumed that they are based on unalterable characteristics. The fact of the matter is that to say that an individual falls into a certain typology need be no more stereotyping than to say that the individual has an IQ at a certain level. The IQ may be used as a stereotype but it need not be, as a typology need not be. Whether personality typologies involve unalterable characteristics is an open question. Thus far we know that some individuals can and do change while others cannot and do not change. Only as we gather more data can we answer this question.

Up to this point in our discussion of the psychological approach we have concentrated primarily on the contribution of several substantive areas to the prediction of college success. There are, however, several general points that require highlighting or emphasis.

It is apparent from the studies reviewed in this section that when the personality tests used are effective predictors that they contribute more to the understanding of the characteristics of students who succeed in varying degrees in college than is the case when other approaches to prediction are used. When one has information on the relationship between maladjustment, anxiety, need achievement, and so forth, one has a greater appreciation of the kinds of psychological factors that may impede or facilitate a student in his capacity to take advantage of the stimuli he is exposed to in his college environment than is the case if one is limited to such data as high school rank, geographical location of residence, parents' education, and so forth. The personality data tell us about the student as he himself is at the time he is in college and not about others with whom he might have been associated (as was true in the social or demographic approach) and from which one has to infer the student's characteristics.

At several points in this monograph, it was suggested that predictive studies that increase our understanding have several advantages over those that do not. For one, they tell us something of the kinds of students that are produced in college. For example, it appears from several studies reviewed that conformity may be an important psychological characteristic to possess if one wants to succeed in some colleges. And, such a finding might well stimulate the thinking of educators. Another advantage of studies that provide understanding is that the data may be used in counseling students. Thus, it is conceivable that with knowledge of the relationships between maladjustment and college success efforts might be devoted to aiding students to overcome their difficulties and thus adjust more effectively to their college environments. A third advantage that was suggested is that knowledge of the students' personality characteristics might well be an aid to the development of teaching techniques that are appropriate to the students' characteristics.

It is no doubt likely that these possible advantages have been made use of in some college situations although, to our knowledge, there are no descriptions in the literature of how data collected in assessment or predictive studies have been used systematically for such purposes. With regard to one of the advantages suggested previously, the utilization of teaching techniques that are appropriate to the students' characteristics, there is a study (Stern, 1960, 1962) which illustrates the idea we have in mind. Although the study falls short of the goal in that specific teaching techniques were not developed beforehand, it nevertheless has the advantage of illustrating what might be done in terms of the experiences of a sensitive observer.

Previously (p. 28) we discussed the characteristics of three types of individuals that may be found among student groups — Stereopaths, Non-Stereopaths, and Rationals. To gather additional data on the classroom behavior of these types of students, Stern set up three special sections in a class on citizenship for freshmen at Syracuse University. One class was composed exclusively of authoritarian students (Stereopaths), the second exclusively of nonauthoritarians (Non-Stereopaths), and the third exclusively of Rationals. All sections were taught by the same instructor who was unaware of the criteria involved in selecting the students. Each class met once a week throughout the semester and the instructor kept a diary of what took place during the class sessions.

During the first two class meetings the instructor commented that the authoritarians were "lacking in curiosity or initiative . . . direct questioning required to get class discussion and there was much less interplay between the students"; the nonauthoritarians "have a bargaining, critical attitude [although] not exactly hostile . . . many questions on details of course administration"; the Rationals impressed him as "obviously all the future campus leaders . . . very responsive but friendly. There were some questions on the administration of the course but they were not pointed or sharp."

By the end of the third class session the instructor's initial evaluation of the authoritarian class does not change but his reactions to the other two do. Of the authoritarians he says, "Very difficult to get discussion, although direct questions indicate they are well informed on the text . . . a constant temptation to 'lecture' rather than discuss. . . ." About the nonauthoritarians he comments, "This class is becoming my delight. They take nothing for granted, yet their criticism and controversy is friendly. . . ." And of the Rationals he feels, "This group is going to seed, and it is probably my fault. They seem to have a sense of self-assurance and security, and a 'we can't lose out' kind of confidence. . . . I cannot to date get anything but bland cooperation: creative, critical thought, or self-criticism is hard to find here. . . ."

We can interrupt the instructor's description of the students' behavior at this point because it is quite characteristic of them. Their behavior as described above is also consistent with Stern's experiences with these types in previous research. The critical group for our purposes is the authoritarian group and as Stern had previously learned they do not like the citizenship course and indeed they usually do not do well in it. Indeed, at the same time that the three special sections were being taught there were other students assigned in random fashion to other citizenship sections. The data on the authoritarian students assigned to the other classes indicated that they did much more poorly in class than their other classmates. But, the significant point is that the authoritarians assigned to the special section did not do poorly. As a matter of fact, they did just as well as the nonauthoritarians and the Rationals in the other two special sections with the same instructor. Furthermore, the latter two types of students did just as well as their counterparts in the nonexperimental sections so the fact that the authoritarians did as well as the nonauthoritarians or the Rationals could not be attributed to the instructor's general superiority. "Nor was this improvement in performance for the authoritarians in the experimental class associated with any unique changes in ideology."

Why did the authoritarians in the experimental section do as well as the other two groups in the citizenship class? Why did they do better than the other authoritarians that were assigned at random to other classes? What seems to have made the difference was the instructor's teaching technique. Here, it is worthwhile to quote at length from Stern (1962).

"The diary provides a clue to experiences that may have been responsible for this outcome. The instructor emphasizes in many different ways that his primary objective was to stimulate the free exchange of ideas. . . .

"Throughout the semester, however, he continues to press for discussion with the latter two sections (authoritarians and Rationals). During the first month he continually refers to the effort to get these sections to respond. Several techniques stand out: (a) continued pressure from him, in the form of direct questions, (b) a refusal on his part to lecture or to provide direct answers, (c) his encouragement and acceptance of any response from the students, and (d) his insistent adoption of absurdly extreme positions. . . ."

It was the last technique that seemed to have turned the tide with the authoritarian and Rational students. When the issue of slavery came up for discussion in the class the instructor adopted the extreme positive of favoring "slavery," that is, putting the mob in any civilization into its place—"so you intelligent folks can operate a *good* democracy."

This was the turning point, and from here on in the class discussions became more satisfactory. The instructor now notes in his diary that: The authoritarian class gave "evidence in more individual cases of willingness to fight back against the brutally dogmatic totalitarian rantings of the professor. I tried to seduce them to totalitarianism, and they indignantly, but politely, told me I was wrong." The class of Rationals "too, including many previously silent, attacked my theories on slavery. The happiest thing appears to be that many of them now are apparently deciding that it is o.k. to disagree, verbally brawl with, and slap the prof in his place." For the nonauthoritarians, the instructor reports ". . . the period came to an end too quickly."

Stern summarizes this study by saying, "The significance of this study does not lie in the use of the discussion method as an educational panacea, but rather in the effect that the persistent application of particular discussion techniques had in helping a group of authoritarian students increase their knowledge in an area to which they are usually resistant.

"For the nonauthoritarians the experiment described here was superfluous; they showed no gains, and succeeded mainly in demonstrating a competence they had already enjoyed prior to taking the course. The Rationals also showed no gains, although their failure was not in their mastery of the course materials but in terms of a more personal objective set by the instructor himself. Viewed against general education objectives, the authoritarians were the only clearly deficient and difficult group of students, and the only ones to have been clearly responsive to the specialized techniques to which they had been exposed in their own isolated classroom environment."

Although the material presented is based on only one set of experiences, one cannot help but think of the value of future systematic research in this area for the development of teaching techniques that would take into account the personalities of the students. Is it too much to expect that as such information is assembled classes of students might be formed on the basis of personality data, just as intelligence tests are used for similar purposes in some elementary school situations?

Having discussed some of the functions that the psychological approach to prediction based on personality data might serve, let us now turn to several comments about methodological and procedural matters that require further emphasis.

Researchers in this area need to be cautioned against concentrating solely on the investigation of possible linear relationships that might exist between personality variables and some criterion of college success. While such relationships may exist for certain variables they need not necessarily be obtained for all variables. Unfortunately we do not have sufficient knowledge as yet to say on any *a priori* basis what kind of relationship we might anticipate between a personality variable and a criterion. Consequently, it would be of value, if only as a precaution, to study a scatter plot of the data to determine the character of the distribution of the test scores. Such study would not only indicate what kind of correlational technique to use but it would also reveal how the relationship between variable and criterion might vary as a function of test score. For a good illustration of this point the reader is referred to Sarason and Mandler's (1952) study referred to previously.

Along these same lines it is of value to differentiate between *optimal* and *maximal* test scores. At times one has the impression that when certain personality variables are related to college success the investigator expects that a student with a higher score will be the more successful. Such an attitude is quite consistent with experiences in achievement testing and, no doubt, is a carry-over from this area. In the personality area, however, it is quite possible that a student with a maximal score will be less effective than one with a lower score. A maximal score on certain personality variables might reflect an intense or compulsive quality of the need or the possibility that the need serves a variety of psychological functions. An individual with a maximal test score may therefore be involved in a condition of psychological stress which would make it difficult for him to perform effectively in a learning situation. On the other hand, an individual who has obtained an optimal score may, in all likelihood, perform with greater effectiveness because his score may indicate that he possesses motivation appropriate to the task and that it is not so intense as to override the effective utilization of other psychological functions, especially the intellectual ones. An illustration of this point may be found in the study of Worrell (1959).

The problem, however, is a rather complex one. First, as indicated previously, not all personality variables bear the same relationships (linear or nonlinear) with a criterion. Second, the obtained relationships with the same personality variable may vary as a function of the technique used in gathering the data. For example, some of the studies reviewed on the relationship between need achievement and college success suggest that it is fairly reasonable to expect that a high score on the test will be positively related to the criterion. Worrell's (1959) study, on the other hand, indicates that the student with a high level of aspiration is less likely to do well in terms of grades than a student with a moderate level of aspiration. It is therefore possible that, at least for need achievement, a paper and pencil or objective test measure may yield results where maximal scores are positively related to the criterion, but when projective procedures or when procedures allowing for the operation of fantasy are used, then one would expect optimal scores to yield the best relationships. Whether this is so or not is a problem for future research.

It is quite characteristic of much research in this area that investigators concentrate on the relationship between a single personality variable and some criterion of college success. Such studies are valuable, especially if conducted in line with the suggestions presented above. However, if research stops at this point then our understanding and capacity to predict college success will be limited. Individuals do not behave as the manifestations of single variables. They are better described as possessing a constellation of interacting variables. This issue is most apparent in the study of the relationship between anxiety and college success where it has been pointed out that data are needed not only about a student's anxiety but also about his defense mechanisms. However, the issue can be stated more broadly as one involving the need for the development of an effective classification system of personality variables which will allow for the determination of types of persons based on a variety of characteristics.

It is implicit in the above that we need renewed interest in persons to go hand in hand with the interest in tests that has been quite common in studies in this area. Along with this renewed interest in persons, we might have to alter our orientation regarding another matter that has been carried over from the psychometric tradition. In keeping with the psychometric tradition one is primarily concerned with the development of reliable and valid tests. The attitude that is to be encouraged in line with the previous suggestion is that there be an increased interest in determining who those individuals are who yield valid and reliable results. There is an interaction effect between test and individual. For some individuals a test may predict quite well but the same test with another group of individuals may fall short of its mark. An example of the effect was evident in the review of the study by Frederiksen and Melville (1954) in which it was found that an interest score would predict effectively for noncompulsive students but not for compulsive ones. Under such circumstances a psychological variable may serve as a moderator variable, as suggested by Saunders (1956). One needs to be alert to the effects of these moderator variables and to incorporate them into the constellations that characterize the types of persons to be found in the population studied. As one moves along in line with this suggestion the emphasis is not on what combination of test scores predict well, but rather on what combination of test scores predict well for what kinds of individuals.

As we increase our interest in persons, we should not overlook the fact that these persons are behaving in the context of specific social environments, colleges. Colleges vary along several dimensions as do all social organizations. To be successful in a social organization requires that the individual possess those characteristics that enable him to fulfill environmental demands. This raises at least three points that need to be considered in our future efforts.

First, there are a number of studies that suggest that a student to be successful in college needs to be a conforming individual. However, it is also apparent that not all colleges are such closed systems and that there are colleges, or even subsystems within a "conforming college," that encourage the growth, autonomy, and creativity of their students. Hopefully, such "open system" colleges will become more prevalent. If such be the case then what we shall need are better procedures than are currently used for investigating the constructive or "anabolic" aspects of personality which will aid us in finding the autonomous and creative student, or the student who is capable of change and capable of availing himself of the constructive opportunities provided him by his college. In this regard there may be potential usefulness in the data and techniques developed by Barron (1958), MacKinnon (1959a, 1959b), Roe (1952), and Stein (1962a, 1962b) in their studies of creativity and in the theoretical contributions of Erikson (1953), Hartmann (1958), Sanford (1962), and White (1952, 1960).

A second point that requires our attention as we concentrate on the student in the social context of his college, is the need for test measures that focus more directly on the manner in which personality variables may be manifest in the college situation, and the need for test measures that would tell us how the student perceives the college situation. For example, one of the reasons why a measure of need achievement may not correlate as high as we would like with a criterion of college success is that the student may not perceive the college environment as a situation in which he can be achieving. Indeed, a student may obtain a high score on a test but in terms of his perception of his college environment it may not be the place in which to manifest this need. The test may still be quite valid, for the student may manifest his need achievement in other than college situations. But without information on his perception of his college, one's prediction may be off the mark. Another illustration of this same point involves the relationship between anxiety and academic success. A student may obtain a high score on a measure of anxiety but it may not affect his grades because college, for him, may not be anxiety provoking. Indeed, for him, it is quite a secure place where he gets much satisfaction out of demonstrating his intellectual capacities. It is only when he is in other environments or other relationships that this student may feel anxious. Similarly, another student may score low on a test of anxiety for, indeed, in most situations he is not anxious. He, however, may become anxious in school. Without techniques that focus directly on such matters we might lose sight of critical considerations and transactions. An important step in the direction of what is suggested here is the research by Sarason and Mandler (1952).

The third major point that we need to bear in mind as we consider the student in his social context is the criterion of college success. Investigators in this area are quick to accept easily available criteria such as grades and to correlate them with available test measures. There is nothing necessarily wrong with grades as a criterion but in making such a selection, or in selecting any criterion of college success, it is important to determine what psychological functions or characteristics a student needs to possess if he is to attain the criterion. In other words one needs a functional analysis of the criterion whether it be for the immediate college situation or for an environment in which the student will find himself at some future date. As more data are gathered on the functional analyses of different criteria it may also be possible to integrate in a more adequate fashion some of the conflicting results that may be found in contemporary literature. As an aid to this problem researchers might well consider the transactional approach to assessment to which we now turn.

The transactional approach

The fourth approach to the prediction problem is the transactional approach.* Basic to this approach is the assumption that success in college, as all behavior, is a function of the transactions between the individual and his environment. Individuals affect and are affected by their environments. Consequently, for purposes of prediction it is important to understand both the characteristics of the individual and the environment.

Unlike the other approaches considered thus far, the transactional approach comes directly to grips with the criterion problem, and in so doing makes an important decision between a *standard of performance* and a *criterion*.

A standard of performance is that level or quality of achievement that an individual is said to have attained by significant others. Thus, grades assigned by teachers are standards of performance, just as when teachers rate some students as potentially superior, these students are said to have achieved or manifested certain standards of performance. In the transactional approach then, a standard of performance is what is regarded in more traditional studies as the criterion. The criterion, however, in the transactional approach is composed of those psychological characteristics that an individual needs to possess if he is to achieve the standard of performance.

*Various methods for following this approach are presented by Stern, Stein, and Bloom (1956).

Assessors using the transactional approach believe that psychologists should confine themselves to measuring psychological characteristics. This is their stock in trade. If these characteristics are related to the standard of performance then valid measures of the psychological variables will result in highly predictive results.

Therefore, in the transactional approach the assessor seeks to determine what the psychological requirements are that are imposed on the individual by the environment. These requirements or prerequisites are collated into a "model." Techniques and procedures which are expected to cast light on whether or not an individual possesses these requirements are then selected for use. Students are studied with these techniques and the degree of congruence between the student and the model is established. If the student fits the model, he is regarded, *ipso facto*, as successful in the situation. If he does not, then he is not regarded as successful.

In a sense it may be said that the model is constantly tested and revised. Success in predicting is taken as an indication of how accurate the model is. However, inadequate predictions may also result from errors made in deciding what tests or procedures to use or in analyzing test results. It is important to stress this last point for in any prediction study one may make errors in diagnosing or understanding the student, or in predicting his behavior, or both (O.S.S. Assessment Staff, 1948). And, it is critical to try to understand which has been made.

To illustrate what occurs in the transactional approach we shall cite experiences in two studies conducted by Stern, Stein, and Bloom (1956).

In the first study the task was to differentiate between students regarded as ideal and students regarded as undesirable in a midwestern seminary. On the basis of information collected from the faculty the following theoretical model of the ideal student was developed.

1. *Interpersonal relations.* Includes capacity for involvement with others, the ability to interact skillfully with peers, superiors, and subordinates, without arousing hostility or rejection. Such rapport will involve social sensitivity, tact, and confidence in social contact. Aggressive impulses should be well socialized, and the individual should appear as autonomous rather than dependent or dominant.

2. *Inner state.* Characterized by high energy, consistently and purposively directed.

3. *Goal orientation.* Will be persistent in attacking problems, although not inflexible. When confronted with possible failure, the individual will counteract, restriving in order to overcome obstacles, rather than withdrawing or otherwise avoiding the issue. Although primarily intraceptive, the student will focus on people and personal relations. The structure under consideration here, referred to previously in the conceptual framework . . . as *Exocathection-Intraception*, involves dramatic, idealistic social action, active modification of reality to conform to a private value-system, and the expression of ideals in concrete action. The content of this structure should be sociopolitical as well as ethical-religious.

Six students, three at either extreme were then selected and studied with the following instruments: Wechsler-Bellevue Test of Adult Intelligence, Rorschach Test, Thematic Apperception Test, Sentence Completion Test, and an Autobiographical Questionnaire.

Intelligence test measures did not differentiate between the students, IQ scores ranged from 128 to 143 and there were no significant differences among the scatter patterns. The remainder of the test battery was analyzed clinically to determine whether the student possessed a personality pattern that was or was not congruent with the aforementioned model.

All six students were correctly placed as ideal or undesirable. But the assessment did not end here for it was possible on the basis of the clinical analyses to gain appreciable understanding of the two groups. Thus, of the three who were congruent with the personality model the authors say, "These three appeared to be capable of maintaining a façade in social contact similar to our initial specifications. Feelings of hostility were generally in control for this group, or channeled into socially acceptable forms of behavior. All three would appear autonomous and independent, although it was noted that for one student this might well be merely the surface appearance of an essentially narcissistic individual. Energy level was high for these three students, and accompanied by high goals and counteractive restriving. Finally, all three individuals were predominantly intraceptive, coupled with a cathexis of external factors that are chiefly social. Although introspection and inner soul-searching were not entirely lacking, energy was expended primarily on the active influencing of situations and people along lines dictated by a private system of values.

"It was further brought out in the assessment conferences that the other three subjects differed markedly from the model, and to some extent from one another. Social relations ranged from attempted dominance to strained uneasiness. All three lacked insight or sensitivity to others. Although energy level was high, much was lost by all three as a result of anxiety and tension. Only one of the three could be called counteractive; a second appeared to respond to frustration with extra-punitiveness, while the third was more perseverative than persistent. An exocathective intraceptive structure (idealistic social action) somewhat similar to that specified in the model characterized one, although the emphasis in this case was more upon compulsive introspection and metaphysical speculation than upon social action as indicated in the model. The other two could be more accurately described in terms of exocathection-extraception: the manipulation of external objects through concrete acts for more or less immediately tangible ends. Status, security, and community recognition seemed to constitute the major source of their motivations for the ministry."

Thus, using the transactional approach, it was possible not only to post-dict accurately but also to obtain a great deal of understanding concerning the characteristics of students who were capable of fulfilling the standard of performance and those who

were not.

It was indicated previously that one of the problems in predicting behavior is the possibility of confusing errors in diagnosis with errors in prediction. Thus, for example, it is possible for the psychologist to make a very accurate diagnosis of the student's personality or to have a very complete understanding of the student. Even when this is so, however, one may not predict accurately because one may not be aware of the extent to which the environment, or specifically the significant others, may be willing to tolerate deviations from the model. In the traditional approach such information may be lost so that the psychologist loses important data on the basis of which he may be able to correct his mistakes. Due to the feedback relationship between psychologists and significant others in the transactional approach there is opportunity to take advantage of certain safeguards from which one might profit in the future. How this happens is reflected in the second study in which the subjects were teacher-trainees.

One of the purposes of the teacher-trainee study was to overcome a limitation of the seminary study. In the seminary study only extreme groups were studied. In the teacher-trainee study the entire student body consisting of 10 students was selected. A hypothetical model of a successful student was developed and the entire student body of 10 students was rank-ordered in terms of success. The students were studied with the same battery used with the seminary students and each student's case was compared for congruence with the model. The correlation between the faculty's rank order and the assessor's rank order resulted in a correlation of $+.70$ significant at the .02 level. All but two students were ordered correctly and study of the two that were misplaced resulted in further understanding.

In the case of one student, "the assessment staff had considered energy level and counteraction to be very high, as was the need for affiliation, but associated with underlying feelings of hostility. Such feelings were not expressed, however, but held in check by means of rigid conformity and a compulsive drive for achievement, both associated with considerable anxiety. These defensive characteristics were taken by the assessment staff to have positive adaptive value in this situation, apart from their function within a neurotic structure. The faculty did not disagree with this evaluation . . . on the contrary they indicated in the conferences that they had in effect already recognized the neurosis and rejected the student.

In the second case a reversal of this situation occurred. "The assessors felt that a great deal of latent instability was indicated, making prognosis poor despite many superficial similarities with the criterion model. The faculty, it was learned subsequently, had chosen the student as successful on admittedly slender evidence; the student was a newcomer to the program who had been chosen because of her experience with children in a Sunday school class, and the apparent strength of her goals in teaching."

The two studies just presented were conducted in terms of the analytic method. In this there is much communication between faculty and psychologists early in the research so that the best model may be constructed. After the students are studied and the post-dictions are made, faculty and psychologists meet again to evaluate the results. The amount of time spent with faculty at this point depends on what refinements in the model need to be developed and the degree of feedback desired by the faculty. In the analytic method the psychologists may use a variety of procedures but in the work described by Stern, Stein, and Bloom (1956) heavy weight was placed on clinical procedures and projective techniques which require a fairly high degree of sophistication. This method is best used with a small group of students and because of the time required of faculty and students, and because of the degree of sophistication required on the part of the psychologists, this method is rather expensive.

To cut down on the expense involved and to make it possible to study larger numbers of students Stern, Stein, and Bloom present three additional assessment methods—empirical, synthetic, and configurational. The empirical approach involves the selection of a standard of performance and the study of the relationship between it and the tests administered. A model is built and refined and post-dictions made. This process is continued until appropriate levels of prediction are obtained.

The synthetic approach stems from an abstract analysis of the good performer. The psychologist on the basis of his theoretical knowledge of personality or his knowledge of the situation hypothesizes that a certain kind of individual will do well or poorly in the situation. A test is constructed to find just this kind of student and his standard of performance is then studied.

The configurational approach involves the administration of a battery of tests and the use of appropriate statistical procedures (for example, inverse factor analysis) to determine the psychological patterns in the test data.

Comparing all four approaches we find that the analytic method is most time-consuming and most expensive. It also provides most understanding of the students and therefore has most value for feedback to faculty and counseling for students. The other three approaches are less expensive and in turn provide less understanding of the student but more than is available with traditional approaches.

All four approaches are highly dependent on the cooperation and involvement of faculty and the capacity and ingenuity of psychologists.

The transactional approach has not been used very much, possibly because of the difficulties of developing models of the environment. Recent developments augur well for its more frequent use. Stern and Pace (1958) have developed a procedure for studying the college environment which may be used separate from or in conjunction with the Activities Index developed by Stern (1958). The advantage of using both these procedures together is that they are both based on Murray's system of need-press analysis (Murray, 1938). Stein (1959a, 1959b, 1962a) has used a system of role analysis in his study of creativity which makes it possible to learn about the role

requirements for scientists in industry from which one may then infer the psychological characteristics the individual needs to possess. It is possible that this method, with modification, may be applied to other situations.

Summary

The purpose of this monograph was to investigate the role of antecedent and personality factors in the prediction of college success. To fulfill this purpose a sample of the literature published during 1950 to 1960 was surveyed.

There were many ways in which the literature might have been integrated. One might have concentrated on substantive results, on procedures utilized, or on characteristics of the populations studied. However, it was felt that future research efforts could be best facilitated through highlighting the different approaches that have been used and the extent to which each of them contributes to the goals of all research—*understanding and prediction*. In the course of this presentation substantive findings were also indicated.

Four major approaches characterize current efforts to predict college success on the basis of antecedent and personality factors. They are: the pilot experience, the social and demographic approach, the psychological approach, and the transactional approach.

The pilot experience approach banks on the similarity between the high school and college experience and thus uses measures of high school achievement (grades or ranks) to predict success in college. When high school grades or ranks are used, especially when used with appropriate correction factors that take into account differences between institutions, rather high correlations (in the range of +.70 to +.80) between high school achievement and college success are obtained. However, it is only when such studies also include an investigation of personality factors that we obtain more complete understanding of why the aforementioned correlations have been obtained. While this understanding is currently based on studies of high level students it nevertheless suggests that conformity is an important ingredient in achieving college success. This in turn suggests that the college experience may well be regarded as a continuation of socialization processes in our processes.

The advantage of the pilot experience approach is that it concerns itself with data which are relatively easy to obtain. But, it is subject to problems of lag and adaptation. It takes time to build up normative data. If classes are selected in terms of high school grades homogeneous populations may be developed and the restricted range of population plus differential grading systems in college may diminish the level of obtained correlations. This approach also does not allow for dealing with new high schools for which no information is available nor does it cope adequately with the problem of the "late-bloomers."

The social and demographic approach may be said to be based on the thesis that history makes the man. It concerns itself with the characteristics of others with whom the student has been associated or with the characteristics of situations over which the student has had no control. The effects of these circumstances on the student are inferred from data available in other sociopsychological or sociological studies but their presence is not necessarily tested directly.

Again, this approach has the advantage that social and demographic data are rather easily available and obtainable. However, as it is presently used it overlooks the *functional equivalence* and *functional significance* of social factors for the individual. Data obtained with this approach may encourage the development and utilization of stereotypes and prejudices in the selection of college students for it does not highlight *characteristics of the student* but *attributes of the environment* from which he comes. As currently used this approach is rather limited in predicting college success but its value may be increased if it were to concentrate on the dynamics of antecedent factors. In this regard the works of Roe (1957) and Stein (unpublished) on parent-child relationships and later adult patterns of interests and creativity were cited as of potential significance.

If the social or demographic approach may be said to assume that history makes the man, then the third approach discussed, the psychological approach, may be said to assume that man makes history. The psychological approach, as used here, refers to the relationships between early parent-child transactions and later development and to the current personality characteristics of the individual. With regard to early parent-child relationships, it was suggested that studies in the area of creativity might make valuable contributions to furthering our understanding of what makes for college success. Since these studies concentrate on the dynamics of the parent-child transaction they overcome some of the shortcomings of the social and demographic approach.

As was said previously, the psychological approach also concerns itself with the current personality characteristics of the student. Among the studies surveyed a variety of personality factors have been studied including over-all adjustment, anxiety, control and compulsiveness, need achievement, masculinity and femininity, and typological characteristics. Among the techniques that have been used to study the students' personality characteristics there are objective tests, projective tests, questionnaires, and experimental situations.

With regard to over-all adjustment, the results obtained with projective tests appear to be not as differentiating nor as consistent as those obtained with objective tests. Among the objective tests the MMPI appears to be most efficient in differentiating between groups of students that differ in academic success. The more successful students are less maladjusted in terms of deviation from a norm than are the less successful ones.

Theoretically, anxiety may either serve to increase the drive to achievement or it may serve to disrupt goal-oriented behavior. However, anxiety as measured by a test of manifest anxiety has not been found to be related to college success when used alone. It may be more useful when combined with other measures of control and commitment to college. More information is needed on the nature of students' maladjustments and anxieties so that more adequate plans to help students with these difficulties can be developed. It was also suggested that researchers might well pay more attention to the significance of different types of anxieties, the defense mechanisms related to them, the relevance of the anxieties to the college situations, and the students' attitudes to their problems.

Another of the substantive findings covered in this survey was that excessively controlled and rigid students (as defined by a measure of stereopathy) differ from their less controlled and less conforming classmates in placement tests, learning outcomes, vocational preferences at the time of entering college, in their classroom behavior, in the evaluations they receive from their instructors, and in their adjustment to college. The Stereopath student did less well in tests, involving verbal facility, flexibility, and skill in analysis than his Non-Stereopath classmate. The Stereopath also did less well in adjusting to college and in the ratings he obtained from his instructors than did the Non-Stereopath. These results, however, were obtained in a college environment that was opposed to rigidity and conventionality. Under certain conditions where the criterion is such that conformity is a virtue the Stereopath is likely to do better than the Non-Stereopath.

It was also pointed out in discussing compulsiveness that the noncompulsive student is more predictable with interest inventories than is the compulsive student. This led to the suggestion that a major issue in this area is to determine what kinds of students are predictable with what kinds of techniques under what kinds of circumstances.

The evidence on need achievement generally indicated that it served best in prediction when used in conjunction with measures of control and commitment to college. The discussion of studies of achievement motivation suggested the importance of concerning oneself with whether the student perceives the college situation as an appropriate environment for manifesting his achievement drive and whether the student has the capacity to adapt his drive to the college situation. Our discussion also pointed to the importance of differentiating between maximal and optimal test scores for predictive purposes and to the significance of differentiating the conditions under which projective and objective measures of needs are most valuable for predictive purposes.

Masculinity and femininity have also been studied and in general it has been found that for male students, high scores on femininity are more important for college success, and for female students, masculinity appears to be a critical variable. For males, high scores on femininity were also found to be critical when combined with other personality factors. It was suggested that terms such as cultural interests or aesthetic interests might well be substituted for the terms masculinity-femininity as used in predictive studies. Also, if there is an interest in studying masculinity and femininity then these should be regarded as two separate factors and not as extremes of a continuum in light of theoretical considerations which point to the bisexual character of human beings. Then, too, it was pointed out that there is much needed research in this area that might explore the value of nonobjective measures of masculinity and femininity and their potential usefulness when combined with other measures.

Finally, in the psychological approach we also find studies that concern themselves with patterns of personality characteristics or typologies. These studies are based on the assumption that a class of students is composed of different kinds of students whose personalities are manifest in a complex of variables. This assumption is congruent with the theoretical concept of equipotentiality which says that different kinds of individuals may achieve the same goal by following different pathways. The goal may have different significance for these different types of persons. This emphasis on typologies appears to have much value not only for the prediction of college success but also as a basis for forming classes that may be most responsive to different kinds of teaching procedures.

The last approach described in this survey is the transactional approach. It is based on the assumption that college success, as is true of all behavior, is a function of the transactional relationship between the individual and his environment. Unlike the other three approaches it starts with the analysis of what is traditionally called a criterion and names it a *standard of performance accepted by others*. Analysis of what is required, psychologically, on the part of the individual to achieve a standard of performance is regarded as constituting the criterion. The criterion is manifest in a hypothetical model of the successful student and the student is studied to determine whether he possesses characteristics congruent with the model. Congruence then represents suc-

cess and incongruence the lack of it.

The transactional approach has greatest potential for prediction and understanding both for faculty and students. It is not used much currently possibly because of the difficulties of developing models and the problem of gathering related psychological data. Recent developments by Stern and Pace (1958) and Stein (1959a, 1959b, 1962a) for studying the environment, and the Activities Index developed by Stern (1958) and his colleagues which is directly applicable to college students may provide the means to cope with this problem in the future.

Conclusion

Having surveyed a sample of research published during 1950-1960, I should like to discuss two items. The first is in the nature of a hopefully feasible recommendation—the establishment of a clearinghouse for research. The second is a more general discussion of the prediction problem.

A proposed clearinghouse. As one reads the literature in this area one is struck by the diversity in criteria, procedures used, and populations studied. It is therefore a monumental, if not an impossible, task for any one individual to ferret out all the hardcore facts published information contains which may be useful for predictive purposes. It is also impossible for any one individual to survey the existing literature with an eye to unearthing all the critical gaps in our knowledge and about which we would like more information.

In view of these problems and in view of the fact that this area of research is likely to continue as an active and significant one, it is therefore recommended that a research clearinghouse be established. Such an institution could perform many useful functions. For one, it could be a source of information for researchers. Any researcher could learn from the clearinghouse what had been accomplished with specific techniques and populations in specified college situations. As a result he would be less likely to add redundant information and possibly avoid duplicating others' errors. If he so desired, he could check to see whether the problem he wants to work on has not already been studied and so he would be in a better position to make a unique contribution. Furthermore, if the need arose for the utilization of techniques to deal with practical problems in selection, there would be a source the investigator could turn to for information, on the basis of which he would make the wisest decision under the circumstances.

In developing its role as a disseminator of information, the clearinghouse would utilize data retrieval methods and high speed computers to provide maximum information in the shortest possible time.

The clearinghouse might also serve the function, either directly or indirectly, of helping to set standards of reporting in the field. It might provide researchers with a systematic method for reporting results. This would not only serve the purpose of appropriate and thorough coding but it might also have the value of reminding the researcher of several analyses of his data that he might have overlooked. This last point may be viewed as too elementary to be mentioned but it does appear to be rather important in this area of research where much of the work seems to be done by graduate students seeking to fulfill their doctoral requirements.

The clearinghouse might also set standards for the use of tests, cross-validation, and criterion analysis. It would also keep an eye on various tests that purport to measure the same kinds of personality characteristics (for example, anxiety and achievement). It would then set standards for the naming of tests and call attention to investigators in the field as to how differences in test definition of the variables may have affected results (Stein, 1957). There is still another function that such a clearinghouse might perform. Psychological tests and procedures are often misused in college situations. There is no need to repeat the malpractices here for they are eminently well discussed in Fishman (1961). Hopefully, the clearinghouse might well take a hand in rectifying some of these problems. Psychological tests and procedures have taken on critical roles in our society especially as they are used in college situations. Under such circumstances, the profession must take on a monitoring function. "If medical procedures applied to the public welfare were in similarly untrained and mistrained hands, a scandal of national proportions would quickly rack the nation, and medical authorities themselves would be among the first to call for improvements and to chart their direction. The psychological profession has been particularly remiss in this connection. Where is the voice that will cry out for higher standards of training and of competence among those who will interpret and implement the scores that mass testing programs generate so profusely? Where are the leaders of psychology who have devised better training programs for this purpose? Some exist but their numbers are few." (Fishman, 1961.)

If the clearinghouse envisioned here ever comes to be, then one might consider staffing it, in part, with a research group of its own. This group would have at least two major areas of activity. One would involve the analysis and integration of data sent to the clearinghouse. For example, after sufficient data have been sent in on comparable populations the research group might carry out factor analyses of the results to determine whether the factors have been replicated. Another type of problem might involve the investigation of the relative values of objective and projective tests for predictive purposes under a variety of conditions.

The second type of activity that the clearinghouse research group might undertake would involve another type of cooperation from participating colleges. The research group, after surveying the type of information it has available, might well find on occasion that certain types of problems have not been adequately studied or that some types of data are lacking on certain kinds of students or for some kinds of colleges. It would then send a request to a college that might supply this information. If the college would cooperate another gap in our knowledge would be filled.

These are only some suggestions as to the functions that a clearinghouse might fulfill. If it ever came into being it would have additional responsibilities. At this point it would seem that only through the cooperation of cooperatively participating colleges and some central agency can we achieve a significant breakthrough on the problems that confront us in the prediction of college success.

The prediction problem. Studies of college success have at least two major goals: to contribute to understanding and to contribute to the solution of the prediction problem. When either of these goals is not attained the study has fallen short of its mark. Our survey of a decade of research has indicated that few studies meet these standards. Those that do are based on small numbers of students or they are based on only one college. If the future is to yield more significant data then several issues need to be attended to.

First and foremost the complexity of the problems needs to be recognized. Behavior in college, like behavior in any situation, is a function of the transactional relationships between the student and his environment.

The student may be described as composed of three major systems: a system of drives, an internalized system of rewards and punishments, and a system of adaptive mechanisms. Each student has his own constellation of factors in each of these three systems. While groups of students may share some of these constellations, no single constellation or group of constellations can characterize all of them.

Colleges are social institutions set up by the society to achieve certain goals. Toward these ends roles are prescribed that members are expected to fulfill. These roles have limits within which the institution will tolerate some deviation. To insure that the roles are fulfilled, however, the college, like any social institution, has a system of rewards and punishments that it utilizes to reinforce behaviors that are consistent with the roles, and ultimately with the goals, that the college was developed to achieve. But, it should be kept in mind that as individuals vary, so do colleges. They vary in goal, role, and reinforcing dimensions.

If the problems involved in characterizing the individual are complex, if the problems involved in characterizing the environment are difficult, then the problem is ever so much more confounded as one thinks about the individual in his environment. Under such circumstances, to expect simple and sovereign solutions is to court disappointment and failure. Yet what we find in our survey is that it is quite characteristic of many of the studies in this area to concentrate on a single variable or one test for the prediction of college success.

Once the complexity of the problem is recognized then several things follow.

To further our understanding and prediction of college success requires individuals who are trained as assessors and who are *problem-oriented* rather than *technique-oriented*. Investigators who are technique-oriented or who are biased for or against certain types of tests, intellectual or nonintellectual, projective or objective, and so forth, will only continue to supply us with partial data and limited information. For problem-oriented assessors the broad statement of the problem is, as has often been stated in the text of the monograph, with what kinds of techniques can we predict the behavior of what kinds of individuals in what kinds of situations. The goal is not to develop the same set of variables for all individuals in all situations but rather the most critical sets of variables that will take into account differences in individuals and differences in situations.

When the goal of assessment is stated in this fashion it soon becomes apparent that there are several critical problems that require resolution before the assessor can completely fulfill his role. These problems do not only confront college assessors but personality theorists, social psychologists, sociologists, and test developers.

What are these problems? To mention only a few they are:

With regard to the psychology of the individual we still need (1) a nomenclature and a classification system that will cover the critical aspects of his drives, his internalized system of rewards and punishments, and his adaptive mechanisms. No science has matured without a system of classification and we are yet to have one that is accepted by all psychologists. (2) We need further efforts in theory that will highlight the critical aspects of the developmental stage through which the college student is developing. (3) We need to learn more about the anabolic functions of personality. We need to know more about the factors that make for or are related to psychological growth and change and how to stimulate and develop these so that the individual can make use of his potentialities. At the present time, comparatively speaking, we know more about those factors that inhibit growth and forestall change—we know more about the catabolic functions than about the anabolic ones. Both are necessary for complete understanding.

When we consider the college environment, our future efforts might be devoted to the following areas: (1) The further exploration of recently developed methods for characterizing the significant characteristics of the college environment, and where these fall short of the mark, to develop new ones. Knowledge of these characteristics are critical for inferring the kinds of psychological characteristics the students need to possess if they are going to fulfill the demands of the college environment and subsequently the kinds of psychological tests that need to be selected for assessment purposes. (2) The determination of how each of the four years of college differ from each other in significant characteristics. Most of the studies in this survey have limited themselves to the freshman year. But college years do differ from each other in content, demands made upon the student, and so forth. Tests administered upon entering college do not predict the whole course of the individual's life. As environmental conditions change, new predictive equations need to be developed. (3) We need to know more about the psychological functions involved in learning different kinds of course material so that appropriate predictive statements can be made for students who major in different areas. (4) We also need to learn more about the various psychological characteristics that are associated with different criteria of college success. Most of the studies covered in this survey have concerned themselves primarily with grades as a criterion of success. But there are possible criteria such as products produced, judgments (other than grades) of teachers and peers, and follow-ups on future accomplishments.

In addition to the two major areas we have just considered there is still a third that requires further study—the psychological techniques used in the prediction of college success. Here there are several needs that still need to be met: (1) The need for additional systematic knowledge of the relationships between objective and projective measures of personality. Hopefully, this knowledge will enable us to better understand what kinds of individuals yield the same results when studied with both types of instruments, and what kinds of individuals yield one result on an objective test and another result on a projective test. This knowledge may also enable us to decide under what conditions either instrument should be selected for predictive purposes. (2) More intense effort needs to be devoted to refining personality tests, especially their reliability and validity. At the present time there is dissatisfaction with the levels of reliability and validity of personality tests as compared to levels obtained from measures of intellectual functioning. What is often overlooked, however, is the vast effort that has been put into the measures of intellectual functioning. If a similar effort were devoted to measures of personality, no doubt higher reliability and validity coefficients than are currently available could be attained. This endeavor should not be limited to determining the reliability of a test instrument but it should broaden its focus to determine the kinds of individuals who yield either reliable or unreliable results. (3) We need further investigation into the relationships between measures of personality and cognitive variables. Where these are highly intercorrelated it is obvious that to use both in the same test battery yields only redundant information. Where the relationships are different we need to inquire whether the personality variables inhibit or facilitate the utilization of intellectual po-

tential. (4) As theoretical developments yield new possibilities we shall also be confronted with the need for new measures of the new personality variables. We would do well to anticipate these needs and to begin focusing our efforts on the anabolic functions of personality or on the individual's capacity for change. (5) With the advent of computers, assessors need no longer limit themselves to one or two tests in their investigations. Now more than ever it is possible to utilize test batteries which can be analyzed in a variety of ways in a reasonable period of time that will yield maximal understanding and maximal effectiveness for predictive purposes. Previously, investigators may have felt discouraged from developing regression equations or typologies because of the time involved in performing statistical analyses. This need no longer be the case and the time saved in analyzing data might well be devoted to thinking through the theoretical and procedural issues mentioned above.

These are only some suggestions as to the direction of future inquiry. Others have been made in the text and, indeed, the reader can think of still others. As we move along in these directions we are likely to come closer and closer to the goal of predicting college success with greater accuracy and increased understanding.

Bibliography

Abelson, R. P. "Sex Differences in Predictability of College Grades," RB-51-8 *Research Bulletin* (March 29, 1951).

Altman, Esther R. "The Effect of Rank in Class and Size of High School on the Academic Achievement of Central Michigan College Seniors Class of 1957," 52 *Journal of Educational Research* (1959), 307-309.

Barron, F. "The Psychology of Imagination," 199 *Scientific American* (1958), 150.

——————. "Complexity-Simplicity as a Personality Dimension," 48 *Journal of Abnormal and Social Psychology* (1953), 163-173.

Barry, C. A., and Jones, Arlynne L. "A Study of the Performance of Certain Freshman Students," 52 *Journal of Educational Research* (1959), 163-166.

Barton, A. H. *Organizational Measurement and Its Bearing on the Study of College Environments* (New York: College Entrance Examination Board, 1961).

Bendig, A. W. "Comparison of the Validity of Two Temperament Scales in Predicting College Achievement," 51 *Journal of Educational Research* (1958), 605-609.

——————. "The Validity of Two Temperament Scales in Predicting Student Achievement in Introductory Psychology," 50 *Journal of Educational Research* (1957), 571-580.

Bendig, A. W., and Klugh, H. E. "A Validation of Gough's Hr Scale in Predicting Academic Achievement," 16 *Educational and Psychological Measurement* (1956), 516-523.

Berger, I. L., and Sutker, A. R. "The Relationship of Emotional Adjustment and Intellectual Capacity to Academic Achievement of College Students," 40 *Mental Hygiene* (1956), 65-77.

Bergeron, W. L. "An Analysis of the Relationship Between Selected Characteristics and Academic Success of Freshmen at the University of Arkansas," 13 *Dissertation Abstracts* (1953), 505.

Blechner, Janet E., and Carter, H. D. "Rorschach Personality Factors and College Achievement," 7 *California Journal of Educational Research* (1956), 72-75.

Bledsoe, J. C. "Success of Non-High School Graduate GED Students in Three Southern Colleges," 28 *College and University* (1953), 381-388.

Bloom, B. S., and Peters, F. R. *The Use of Academic Prediction Scales for Counseling and Selecting College Entrants* (New York: Free Press of Glencoe, 1961).

Boyd, J. D. "The Relative Prognostic Value of Selected Criteria in Predicting Academic Success at Northwestern University," 15 *Dissertation Abstracts* (1955), 1780.

Brown, D. R. "Non-Intellective Qualities and the Perception of the Ideal Student by College Faculty," 33 *Journal of Educational Sociology* (1960), 269-278.

Burnham, Paul S. (Letter dated May 11, 1962.)

Caron, A., and Wallach, M. "Recall of Interrupted Tasks Under Stress: A Phenomenon of Memory or of Learning?" 55 *Journal of Abnormal and Social Psychology* (1957), 372-381.

Carter, H. L. J., and McGinnis, D. G. "Some Factors Which Differentiate College Freshmen Having Lowest and Highest Point-Hour-Ratios," 46 *Journal of Educational Research* (1952), 219-226.

Cattell, R. B., and Drevdahl, J. E. A Comparison of the Personality Profile (16 P.F.) of Eminent Researchers with that of Eminent Teachers and Administrators, and of the General Population," 46 *British Journal of Psychology* (1955), 248-261.

Chahbazi, P. "Use of Projective Tests in Predicting College Achievement," 16 *Educational and Psychological Measurement* (1956), 538-542.

Cooper, J. G. "The Inspection Rorschach in the Prediction of College Success," 49 *Journal of Educational Research* (1955), 275-282.

Cronbach, L. J. "Studies of the Group Rorschach in Relation to Success in the College of the University of Chicago," 41 *Journal of Educational Psychology* (1950), 65-82.

Dahlstrom, W. G., and Welsh, G. S. *An MMPI Handbook* (Minneapolis: University of Minnesota Press, 1960).

Davis, J. A., and Frederiksen, N. "Public and Private School Graduates in College," 6 *Journal of Teacher Education* (1955), 18-22.

Drake, L. E. "Interpretation of MMPI Profiles in Counseling Male Clients," 3 *Journal of Counseling Psychology* (1956), 83-88.

Drake, L. E., and Oetting, E. R. "An MMPI Pattern and a Suppressor Variable Predictive of Academic Achievement," 4 *Journal of Counseling Psychology* (1957), 245-247.

Drevdahl, J. E. "Factors of Importance for Creativity," 12 *Journal of Clinical Psychology* (1956), 12-26.

Drevdahl, J. E., and Cattell, R. B. "Personality and Creativity in Artists and Writers," 14 *Journal of Clinical Psychology* (1958), 107-111.

Edwards, A. L. *Manual for Edwards' Personal Preference Schedule* (New York: Psychological Corp., 1954).

Erikson, E. H. "Growth and Crises of the 'Healthy Personality,'" in C. Kluckhohn, H. A. Murray, and D. M. Schneider (eds.), *Personality in Nature, Society and Culture* (New York: Alfred A. Knopf, Inc., 1953), 2nd edition.

Fishman, J. A. "Social-Psychological Theory for Selecting and Guiding College Students," 66 *American Journal of Sociology* (1961), 472-484.

_____. "The Use of Tests for Admission to College: The Next Fifty Years," in A. E. Traxler (ed.), *Long-Range Planning for Education: Report of 22nd Educational Conference* (Washington, D. C.: American Council on Education, 1957), 74-79.

Franck, Kate, and Rosen, E. "A Projective Test of Masculinity-Femininity," 4 *Journal of Consulting Psychology* (1949), 247-256.

Frederiksen, N., and Gilbert, A. C. F. "Replication of a Study of Differential Predictability," 20 *Educational and Psychological Measurement* (1960), 759-767.

Frederiksen, N., and Melville, S. D. "Differential Predictability in the Use of Test Scores," 14 *Educational and Psychological Measurement* (1954), 647-656.

French, J. W. "Validation of New Item Types Against Four-Year Academic Criteria," 49 *Journal of Educational Psychology* (1958), 67-76.

Gerritz, H. G. J. "The Relationship of Certain Personal and Socio-Economic Data to the Success of Resident Freshmen Enrolled in the College of Science, Literature, and the Arts at the University of Minnesota," 16 *Dissertation Abstracts* (1956), 2366.

Gough, H. G. "The Construction of a Personality Scale to Predict Scholastic Achievement," 37 *Journal of Applied Psychology* (1953), 361-366.

Hartmann, H. *Ego Psychology and the Problem of Adaptation*, trans. by D. Rapaport (New York: International Universities Press, Inc., 1958).

Holland, J. L. "The Prediction of College Grades from Personality and Aptitude Variables," 51 *Journal of Educational Psychology* (1960), 245-254.

_____. "The Prediction of College Grades from the California Psychological Inventory and the Scholastic Aptitude Test," 50 *Journal of Educational Psychology* (1959a), 135-142.

_____. "Some Limitations of Teacher Ratings as Predictors of Creativity," 50 *Journal of Educational Psychology* (1959b), 219-223.

Hood, A. B. "Certain Non-Intellectual Factors Related to Student Attrition at Cornell University," 17 *Dissertation Abstracts* (1957), 2919.

Hoyt, D. P., and Norman, W. T. "Adjustment and Academic Predictability," 1 *Journal of Counseling Psychology* (1954), 96-99.

Iffert, R. E. "Drop-Outs: Nature and Causes; Effects on Student, Family, and Society," *Current Issues in Higher Education* (Washington, D. C.: Association for Higher Education, 1956), 94-102.

Kelly, E. G. "A Study of Consistent Discrepancies Between Instructor Grades and Term-End Examination Grades," 49 *Journal of Educational Psychology* (1958), 328-334.

Kim, K. S. "The Use of Certain Measurements of Academic Aptitude, Study Habits, Motivation and Personality in the Prediction of Academic Achievement," 18 *Dissertation Abstracts* (1958), 150.

Kirk, Barbara A. "Counseling Phi Beta Kappas," 2 *Journal of Counseling Psychology* (1955), 304-307.

Klugh, H. E., and Bendig, A. W. "The Manifest Anxiety and ACE Scales and College Achievement," 19 *Journal of Consulting Psychology* (1955), 487.

Knaak, Nancy K. "A Study of the Characteristics of Academically Successful and Unsuccessful Freshmen Women Who Entered Northwestern University in the Fall of 1954," 17 *Dissertation Abstracts* (1957), 304-305.

Lundin, R. W., and Kuhn, J. P. "The Relationship Between Scholarship Achievement and Changes in Personality Adjustment in Men After Four Years of College Attendance," 63 *Journal of Genetic Psychology* (1960), 35-42.

MacKinnon, D. W. *The Creative Worker in Engineering* (Paper presented at the Eleventh Annual Industrial Engineering Institute, University of California, Los Angeles, and the University of California, Berkeley, February 6-7, 1959a).

_____. "On Becoming an Architect," *Architectural Record* (August 1959b).

_____. *What Do We Mean By Talent and How Do We Test For It?* (Paper read at the Colloquium on Problems and Responsibilities of United States Colleges in the Search for Talented Students, College Entrance Examination Board, Harriman, New York, 1959c).

MacLachlan, Patricia S., and Burnett, C. W. "Who Are the Superior Freshmen in College?" 32 *Personnel and Guidance Journal* (1954), 345-349.

Matarazzo, J. D., Ulett, G. A., Guze, S. B., and Saslow, G. "The Relationship Between Anxiety Level and Several Measures of Intelligence," 18 *Journal of Consulting Psychology* (1954), 201-205.

McArthur, C. C. "Sub-Culture and Personality During the College Years," 33 *Journal of Educational Sociology* (1960), 260-268.

McArthur, C. C., and King, S. "Rorschach Configurations Associated with College Achievement," 45 *Journal of Educational Psychology* (1954), 492-498.

McClelland, D. C. *The Achieving Society* (New York: D. Van Nostrand Co., Inc., 1961).

McClelland, D. C., Atkinson, J. W., Clark, R. A., and Lowell, E. L. *The Achievement Motive* (New York: Appleton-Century-Crofts, 1953).

McClelland, D. C., *et al.* "The Projective Expression of Needs: IV. The Effect of Need for Achievement on Thematic Apperception," 39 *Journal of Experimental Psychology* (1949), 242-255.

Middleton, G., Jr., and Guthrie, G. M. "Personality Syndromes and Academic Achievement," 50 *Journal of Educational Psychology* (1959), 66-69.

Mohandessi, K., and Runkel, P. J. "Some Socioeconomic Correlates of Academic Aptitude," 49 *Journal of Educational Psychology* (1958), 47-52.

Morgan, H. H. "A Psychometric Comparison of Achieving and Nonachieving College Students of High Ability," 16 *Journal of Consulting Psychology* (1952), 292-298.

Mukherjee, C. "Characteristics of Honor Graduates of the University of Nebraska," 18 *Dissertation Abstracts* (1958), 499-500.

Murray, H. A. *Thematic Apperception Test* (Cambridge: Harvard University Press, 1943).

Murray, H. A., *et al. Explorations in Personality* (New York: Oxford University Press, Inc., 1938).

Myers, R. C. "Biographical Factors and Achievement; an Experimental Investigation," RB-50-51 *Research Bulletin* (August 1950).

Nix, Alice P. "An Evaluation of the Contributions of Four Selected Personality Factors to the Prediction of First Quarter Grades of University of Georgia Freshmen in Selected Curricular Areas," 20 *Dissertation Abstracts* (1960), 2678-2679.

O'Connor, J., Lorr, M., and Stafford, J. W. "Some Patterns of Manifest Anxiety," 12 *Journal of Clinical Psychology* (1956), 160-163.

O.S.S. Assessment Staff. *Assessment of Men* (New York: Holt, Rinehart & Winston, Inc., 1948).

Parrish, J., and Rethlingshafer, Dorothy. "A Study of the Need to Achieve in College Achievers and Non-Achievers," 50 *Journal of Genetic Psychology* (1954), 209-226.

Patton, B. K., Jr. "A Study of Drop-Outs from the Junior Division of Louisiana State University, 1953-55," 19 *Dissertation Abstracts* (1958), 484-485.

Peterson, C. A. "A Two-Year Study of Causal Factors in Male Student Drop-Outs at the University of Pittsburgh, 1955-57," 19 *Dissertation Abstracts* (1958), 1255-1256.

Piers, G., and Singer, M. B. *Shame and Guilt* (Springfield, Ill.: Charles C. Thomas, Publisher, 1953).

Roe, Anne. "Early Differentiation of Interests," in C. W. Taylor (ed.), *The Second (1957) University of Utah Research Conference on the Identification of Creative Scientific Talent* (Salt Lake City: University of Utah Press, 1957), 98-108.

————. *The Making of a Scientist* (New York: Dodd, Mead & Co., 1952).

Sanders, Wilma B., Osborne, R. T., and Greene, J. E. "Intelligence and Academic Performance of College Students of Urban, Rural, and Mixed Backgrounds," 49 *Journal of Educational Research* (1955), 185-193.

Sanford, N. "Developmental Status of the Entering Freshman," in N. Sanford (ed.), *The American College* (New York: John Wiley and Sons, Inc., 1962).

————. "Editor's Note on Webster, H. Some Quantitative Results," in N. Sanford (ed.) "Personality Development During the College Years," 12 *Journal of Social Issues* (1956).

Sarason, S., and Mandler, G. "Some Correlates of Test Anxiety," 47 *Journal of Abnormal and Social Psychology* (1952), 810-817.

Saunders, D. R. "Moderator Variables in Prediction," 16 *Educational and Psychological Measurement* (1956), 209-222.

Schachter, S. *The Psychology of Affiliation* (Stanford, Calif.: Stanford University Press, 1959).

Schultz, D. G., and Ricciuti, H. N. "Level of Aspiration Measures and College Achievement," 51 *Journal of Genetic Psychology* (1954), 267-275.

Shuey, Audrey M. "Academic Success of Public and Private School Students in Randolph-Macon Woman's College: I. The Freshman Year," 49 *Journal of Educational Research* (1956), 481-492.

————. "Academic Success of Public and Private School Students at Randolph-Macon Woman's College: II. The Sophomore Year," 52 *Journal of Educational Research* (1958), 35-37.

Sie, Georgiana D. W. "The Relationship of Two Experimental Measures of Student Motivation to Academic Success in College," 15 *Dissertation Abstracts* (1955), 1556-1557.

Sopchak, A. L. "Prediction of College Performance by Commonly Used Tests," 14 *Journal of Clinical Psychology* (1958), 194-197.

Stein, M. I. "Creativity and the Scientist," in B. Barber and W. Hirsch (eds.), *The Sociology of Science* (New York: Free Press of Glencoe, 1962a).

————. *Survey of the Psychological Literature in the Area of Creativity with a View Toward Needed Research*, Cooperative Research Project No. E-3 (Washington, D.C.: U.S. Office of Education, 1962b).

————. *Stein Research Environment Survey* (Chicago: Science Research Associates, 1959a).

————. "Problems Involved in Predictors of Creativity," in C. W. Taylor (ed.), *The Third (1959) University of Utah Research Conference on the Identification of Creative Scientific Talent* (Salt Lake City: University of Utah Press, 1959b), 178-186.

————. "Criteria of Non-Intellectual Aspects of Personality," in *Invitational Conference on Testing Problems* (Princeton, N. J.: Educational Testing Service, 1957).

Stein, M. I., *et al. Social and Psychological Factors Affecting Creativity* (unpublished).

Stern, G. G. "Environments for Learning," in N. Sanford (ed.), *The American College* (New York: John Wiley and Sons, Inc., 1962), 690-730.

————. "Congruence and Dissonance in the Ecology of College Students," 8 *Student Medicine* (1960), 304-339.

————. *Stern Activities Index* (Syracuse: Psychological Research Center, Syracuse University, 1958).

Stern, G. G., and Pace, C. R. *College Characteristics Index* (Syracuse: Psychological Research Center, Syracuse University, 1958).

Stern, G. G., Stein, M. I., and Bloom, B. S. *Methods in Personality Assessment* (New York: Free Press of Glencoe, 1956).

Stone, D. R., and Ganung, G. R. "A Study of Scholastic Achievement Related to Personality as Measured by the Minnesota Multiphasic Personality Inventory," 50 *Journal of Educational Research* (1956), 155-156.

Taylor, Janet A. "A Personality Scale of Manifest Anxiety," 48 *Journal of Abnormal and Social Psychology* (1953), 285-290.

Thompson, Grace M. "College Grades and the Group Rorschach: A Follow-Up Study," 78 *Journal of Genetic Psychology* (1951), 39-46.

Vorhaus, Pauline G. "Rorschach Configurations Associated with Reading Disability," 16 *Journal of Projective Techniques* (1952), 3-19.

Webster, H. "Some Quantitative Results," in N. Sanford (ed.) "Personality Development During the College Years," 12 *Journal of Social Issues* (1956), 29-43.

Weiss, P., Groesbeck, B., and Wertheimer, M. "Achievement Motivation, Academic Aptitude, and College Grades," 19 *Educational and Psychological Measurement* (1959), 663-666.

Weitz, H., and Colver, R. M. "The Relationship Between the Educational Goals and the Academic Performance of Women, a Confirmation," 19 *Educational and Psychological Measurement* (1959), 373-380.

Weitz, H., and Wilkinson, H. Jean. "The Relationship Between Certain Non-Intellective Factors and Academic Success in College," 4 *Journal of Counseling Psychology* (1957), 54-60.

White, R. W. "Competence and the Psychosexual Stages of Development," in M. R. Jones (ed.), *Nebraska Symposium on Motivation* (Lincoln: University of Nebraska Press, 1960).

————. *Lives in Progress* (New York: Holt, Rinehart & Winston, Inc., 1952).

Worrell, L. "Level of Aspiration and Academic Success," 50 *Journal of Educational Psychology* (1959), 47-54.

Yeomans, W. N., and Lundin, R. W. "The Relationship Between Personality Adjustment and Scholarship Achievement in Male College Students," 57 *Journal of Genetic Psychology* (1957), 213-218.